THE GOOD ENOUGH MOTHER

REIMAGINING
MOTHERHOOD & WORK

hilary barnett

This book is dedicated to Evangeline Quinn and Tessa Rose. I want to be just like you when I grow up.

THE JOURNEY

One day you finally knew
what you had to do, and began,
though the voices around you
kept shouting
their bad advice—
though the whole house
began to tremble
and you felt the old tug
at your ankles.
"Mend my life!"
each voice cried.
But you didn't stop.
You knew what you had to do,
though the wind pried
with its stiff fingers
at the very foundations,
though their melancholy
was terrible.
It was already late
enough, and a wild night,
and the road full of fallen
branches and stones.
But little by little,
as you left their voice behind,
the stars began to burn
through the sheets of clouds,
and there was a new voice
which you slowly
recognized as your own,
that kept you company
as you strode deeper and deeper
into the world,
determined to do
the only thing you could do—
determined to save
the only life that you could save.

— Mary Oliver

CONTENTS

INTRODUCTION

Motherhood is cathartic. It is maddening. It is consuming. It takes every ounce of who we are, puts it into a crucible and holds it up as a mirror to our weary eyes. It allows us to see the darkest parts of ourselves and the parts which are the most capable of expanding for love's sake. It stretches us beyond our wildest imaginations and asks us to love to the point of ultimate sacrifice, the kind of love that makes your heart ache and bend in the most uncomfortable directions, the kind of love that grasps but knows it cannot control, the kind of love that gathers but knows that it cannot hold forever.

I so often feel this strange mixture of boredom and frantic activity, like a mouse skittering around its cage, searching for the next sense of pleasure—a cup of coffee, a hit of dopamine from a social media notification, a moment of silence between the wiping of rear ends, the cleaning up of messes, the snuggling, the disciplining, the cooking, the nursing. The overwhelming feeling that being a mom is, cosmically speaking, my most important job. It is an all-consuming job, but I can never shake the feeling it's not the only job I want.

I try to put a noble spin on it and tell myself I want to do something else to be an example to my kids of a strong, empowered woman, but to be quite honest, I have to do it for my own sanity. We all know taking care of kids is challenging, but it is the one thing that we seem to not be able to provide nuance for in public discourse. Mothers are either perceived as whiny and grumbling or simply pretending that motherhood is easy and perfect in every way. Last I checked, it was totally draining and often completely crazy-making. Beautiful? Yes. Magical? Yes. So freaking hard? Yes. So I realize, choosing a double vocation of motherhood and, well, anything else is my attempt to pay attention to the little girl inside me who knew that her story could somehow be magical... could somehow be different.

My daughter loves a show called *Super Why!* In the show, a group of kids "fly" into a fairy-tale book to help the characters out. They actually rewrite the fairy tale to fix the situation—they change the story. My daughter caught onto this pretty quickly. Anytime I asked her to do something she wasn't in the mood to do, she would say, "I can't. It's not in my story."

How often do we sabotage ourselves by automatically assuming that the story we are living is the story we are supposed to be living? Just because it's our current reality doesn't mean it's supposed to be. Rapunzel didn't know how happy she would be outside the tower until she ventured out. Sometimes I think we need a *Super*

Why! team in our own lives to hop in and help us change our story.

We believe so many lies, don't we? We have to be perfect, our kids have to be perfect, we have to decide between our career and our kids, and we can't have it all. But the truth is, we can have it all. We just have to redefine "all." Can we have it all inside systems that reward working sixty-hour weeks until you suffer a catastrophic cardiac event? No. But we can have it all inside of the world we create. The one that values our children, our personal time, and our work as equally important. Instead of constantly striving for perfection, we can embrace being good enough.

Mothers are bombarded from the start: Are you going to breastfeed? Are you going back to work? When? Are you staying home? How long? What do stay-at-home moms do all day? Working moms? It's so sad, they never see their kids. Most moms don't have a choice—we have to earn an income. Staying at home is also a choice that is fraught with our own history of guilt surrounding women's work and domestic labor. What did our mothers do? How much were they home? Did we miss them? Did we feel loved and supported by them?

Every mother has a passion. And it is mothering, and it is also something else. We can be incredible mothers and incredible something else. We must use our education, our resources, and our bravery to make a world that our kids will be thankful to inherit. It's not about climbing ladders or playing by the rules—it's about making our own rules and living by them. It's about honoring what other moms are doing, and recognizing that every single mother has her own unique history, emotions, experiences, and motivations when it comes to how she parents her children.

Right now, I want you to know that I see you. You, on your third cup of coffee, your eyes heavy with the endless sleepless nights, writing a blog post during naptime. You, staying up after the midnight feeding to respond to emails, I see you. You, who just signed the official papers to turn your hobby into something more, I see you. You, mama, who just chose to leave your corporate job to be with your kids, unsure of where the next paycheck will come from, I see you. You, who just this morning dropped your baby off at daycare and sat ugly crying in the parking lot before work, I see you. You, who spent your lunch break pumping in the bathroom stall because you had to go to work after six weeks since your paid leave ran out, I see you. You who just had your first baby and can't imagine ever being able to think straight again. You, mama, working crazy hours just to put food on the table, not sure how you can keep this up. I see you. God sees you. You are doing a great job.

We don't have to choose between loving our kids and chasing our own childhood dreams—we can do both. So many women are, and their stories are not being told. We need to hear of these women who are shaking off the status quo, unraveling other's expectations, choosing their kids and their passion, and saying goodbye to guilt.

In the following chapters, I will introduce the myth that we have all been fed as women and moms—the myth of the perfect mother. As I share my stories and struggles, I want to present another option, another way. The concept of the "Good Enough Mother" was introduced by British pediatrician Donald Winnicott in 1953, and I sincerely believe it can serve us now, as we mother day in and day out. We know that mothers are not one-dimensional, because we have the lived experience of being a mother. We know that mothers are not simply the projection of all our deepest needs, because we know that although we try so hard, we often fail. We are complex, three-dimensional human beings, and that doesn't fold down into one simple and tidy role when our children are born. No, it actually allows us an opportunity to be reborn ourselves and discover (or redefine) who we are at the deepest level. David Winnicott says this:

> *A mother is neither good nor bad not the product of illusion, but is a separate and independent entity: The good enough mother... starts off with an almost complete adaptation to her infant's needs, and as time proceeds, she adapts less and less completely, gradually, according to the infant's ability to deal with her failure. Her failure to adapt to every need of the child helps them adapt to external realities.*

The first thing we must do is face the reality that we will ultimately fail our children. No matter how hard we try, it is inevitable, because we are human. We are fallible, and we struggle. It's that simple. So as we move through the book, hold this idea in your mind—good enough is better than perfect.

When you complete the final page of this book and put it back on your shelf, I hope that you feel seen, understood, and empowered to chase your dreams with your children. Not just as sidekicks, but as part of the amazing, miraculous, and joyous life that you want to build for yourself and your family. I hope you know that the dreams God has placed on your heart from the beginning are sacred, and those beautiful human beings that have been gifted to you are part of the amazing tapestry that God is weaving from your life. I hope you see that your legacy as a mother and an individual holds so much weight, and the choices you make today will reverberate throughout eternity. Perfection is a myth—the beauty lies in the struggle. We were born for such a time as this, and mothering our children has never been a more important task.

CHAPTER 1

LITTLE GIRL, BIG DREAMS

———

... to live in this world

you must be able
to do three things:
to love what is mortal;
to hold it

against your bones knowing
your own life depends on it;
and, when the time comes to let it go,
to let it go.

Mary Oliver, "In Blackwater Woods"

I laid in the hospital bed, IV resting in the crook in my left arm, blood pressure cuff on the other. My eyes stung like fire as I tried to blink the exhaustion away. My legs were anvils binding me to the bed. My lower abdomen was suddenly foreign territory, separated from the rest of me. I couldn't process the violence that had been done under the thin hospital gown. Not right now. I just wanted her in my arms. Bring my baby to me, please.

They carried her in, and the visitors slowly filed out. I unwrapped her sturdy little body from the stiff white blanket and brought her to my chest, shakily. My body surged as she latched on. She was sure of her task, even in my fumbling. Her chin clicked back and forth, her first skill mastered with ease. As her warmth combined with mine, skin on skin, I began to weep silently. You were worth it, baby girl. Every moment.

I always knew I would be a mom.

You know, eventually.

It wasn't something that I thought about at length. It floated around at the edges of my mind—a distant, glimmering future that would eventually make its way into my real life. If you surveyed me at age ten, I would have told you I wanted to be a famous dancer or actress. I was not one of those kids whose Barbie was working hard in the kitchen with her apron waiting for Ken to walk in the door from work. My Barbie was always more of the corporate type.

But I knew, deep down somewhere, I would be a mom, someday. Because that's what women do, right?

Growing up, my parents always told me "you can be anything you want to be!" They met in 1980, both carrying heavy baggage from past relationships and failures. Their love was instant, the kind that sweeps you under. They were married when my mother was two months pregnant with me. It's a running joke, but I like to thank them for inviting me to the wedding. The more sobering aspect of this joke is, they married because of me. They had talked about getting married and having children, but when my mother found out she was expecting, they decided to make a covenant. And they have kept it to this day.

My father worked in straight commission sales most of my life, and he always taught me you had to work for what you made. I always admired my parents for working hard, and I saw them as equals who were earning income as a team. I didn't realize I was part of the "latchkey kid" generation—one that was bemoaned in the media at the time. I never understood why everyone was so concerned about me. I knew my parents loved me deeply, and I also understood that they had to work for us to survive. The two were never mutually exclusive. I would get home from school each day, make myself a snack, and start on my homework. My parents arrived home, dinner was made, and we spent time together. It wasn't the crisis situation that many were making it out to be. At least, not to me.

I never felt sad that my mother worked—I was always so proud of her. She would bring me to her beautiful office in the wing of a historic hospital building, show me her desk, and let me help her set up for workshops. I saw the pictures of students and notes on her wall, so many nurses thanking my mom for helping them get through school. How many people had been nurtured and cared for by these nurses because my mom made it her mission to get them through nursing school with high scores? How many nurses would have failed and never been able to pursue their dreams if it wasn't for my mom? I was in awe of her.

Isn't it fascinating how the stories of our parents weave themselves so powerfully into our own without us even realizing it? Whether we are working to emulate our mothers, working to do the exact opposite, or somewhere in between, so much of how we mother can be a subconscious response to the choices our mothers made.

Even as a young adult, having a family always seemed like something that I would get to eventually. But it didn't factor whatsoever into my career plans. When I pictured my future, I saw myself as one of the leads in a major motion picture—high heels, power suit, espresso in one hand, briefcase in the other. Walking briskly down a hall, West Wing style, I'd have a crowd of staff trailing closely behind me, giving me my schedule for the day and reporting back to me about important results. Then kindly, but with a noblesse oblige air, I'd thank them and enter into my next high-powered meeting. No, I didn't see the allure of a life in the home. I wanted to be "out there," adventuring, conquering, leading, making a dent in the universe.

Of course I wanted a family. Who wouldn't? Of course I wanted the house, the picket fence, the yard. But those were all peripheral to my career. They were part of it, but surely they would just manage to wind their way into my already amazing life, right? Surely.

The powerful women in my family go way back. My paternal grandmother was the essence of a beautiful, strong, and graceful woman. She was the grandma of all grandmas. She was buxom enough to make for a super comfortable pillow to fall asleep on as a small child. I have the happiest memories of sitting on her porch swing with family all around, while she told stories about being sixteen and running away from home to work in a shoe factory in 1924. Even with all the hubbub around me, grownups talking and drinking, I would be lulled to sleep by the sound of her voice. I felt so safe in her lap. My head would rise and fall with her breath, and it would shake when she laughed her deep belly laugh. And now I wonder how she could laugh so deeply. What brought her so much joy?

She had six children and not much money to spare. Her husband worked on trains Midwestern and was gone for long periods, and when he was home, he did his fair share of imbibing. What did she have to get tickled about? But she did. She got tickled and sometimes even peed her pants. The women in my family on both sides have a history of laughing so hard we pee our pants. I think that is an awesome legacy to leave my daughters.

Unfortunately, my grandmother died before she could watch me become a mother myself. What I would have given to hear her secrets—the stories of each of her six children, how they came into the world, what they were like as babies, how she managed to keep it all together. I imagine that for her, mothering in the 1940's through the 1960's, perfection was not even on the radar— survival was the top priority. I would have listened in rapt attention while we sat on her porch swing and she told me everything, the tiniest details that make up the most beautiful and mundane things in a mother's life. They happen in the quiet, in the dark, often. They don't happen in front of an adoring crowd, and great novels have never been written about the glories and tragedies of the life of any mother. We have somehow internalized the message that those tiny moments, those tiny bodies that we care for, day in and day out, do not compete with the majesty and grandeur of life "out there."

And so we don't tell each other our stories. We are left to mother without a real village, without a common understanding, with only algorithms, parenting books, and search engines to help us along. We can do more, and we can do better by each other. We can start by sitting down, around tables, and telling our stories. Recounting the details. The smells, the feeling, the sounds, the emotions, all of it—without shame.

The desire to mother, and the experience of becoming one, completely redefined my sense of self. It is the journey that every one of us begins when we even consider the thought of having children. From the woman who has just begun to have "the itch," to the seasoned mother with grown children, the journey unites us all.

I learned many things the hard way through the process of birthing and raising my daughters, but the one thing I have always wished I could unlearn was that as soon as my children were born, I was being admitted into a larger story—a myth, if you will.

When I welcomed my daughter into the world, I was ushered into the powerful cultural myth of motherhood.

MYTH. MITH/, NOUN

*A traditional story, especially one concerning the early history
of a people or explaining some natural or social phenomenon,
and typically involving supernatural beings or events.*

This motherhood myth holds sway on our everyday
choices, our social circles, our social media groups.

It is the myth that a mother should be perfect.

Not just try hard or do her best- perfection is the
standard, and effortlessness is the mode of operation.

This motherhood myth is rooted in a deep history,
one that we will explore in the following chapters. It is
all encompassing, and it delivers several lies to the new
(and seasoned) mother. The myth whispers that you must
strive, achieve, and please to earn love and acceptance. It
whispers that you are not enough to meet your children's
deepest needs. It sows seeds of comparison, strife, and
resentment. It causes you to question every decision,
in every moment. It produces anxiety and loneliness in
a time when we most need to feel affirmed, connected,
and accepted.

————

Do you feel the ache? I know I do. It's hard to
describe, right? But it's there.

It's there in the exhaustion. Not the kind that sleepless
nights produce, but the soul exhaustion that tells you
things will never change. That tells you she is doing this so

much better than you. That forces you to smile when you want to break down. That shows up in a comment thread when you ask a seemingly innocuous parenting question. It's there, simmering just under the surface, feeding lies and smirking while we scramble to fix ourselves. It turns us toward other mothers in bitterness and accusation, instead of pulling us together.

Birth and mothering are universal- but the myth persists and poisons. It is quiet, subtle. Sometimes the most effective lies are the ones that are covered over in glittering half-truths.

I have been there. I have lived this. I am still walking it out. Motherhood slammed into my preconceived notions about life as I know it, and I have been trying to reconcile this ever since.

I have managed to wade through the darkness and come through the other side with my soul intact. I haven't reached a place of "I get this." I simply have recognized the lies and am choosing every moment to turn toward truth. This book is about us working it out together. It is an experiment in asking hard questions of ourselves, of our society, of the church. It is finding our own *redemption song* in this complex puzzle that is mothering and womanhood and calling. I hope you will walk with me on this journey and we can turn toward the truth and toward each other. The world needs us, our kids need us, and we need this more than ever.

My best friend and I have a special agreement. It's called mom code. When I had my first daughter, we were talking on the phone one day. I started the conversation by saying "I love her so much, but this is just really hard." And my friend quickly corrected me. "You never, ever have to justify your feelings to me. I know you love your daughter. You don't have to convince me of that before you tell me how you are feeling. Just tell me how you are feeling."

That statement caught me completely off guard. I would never want to seem like I was complaining. But it reminded me that our relationship was a judgment-free zone—that no matter what I said to her, she was not going to question my fierce love and devotion to my kids. That I could be painfully honest about the hard things, the scary things, the feelings that I didn't understand, and she would still know I love my daughter. She would still affirm that I am a good enough mom.

Mom code also applies in every other area of life. Did you forget to text someone back right away? It's okay—invoke the mom code. Did you show up late to a playdate? It's okay. Mom code. It's an understanding. A way of saying, "I get it. This is hard. There is grace for you here." And don't we all need that? Don't we all need the ability to be vulnerable without the fear of being judged? As mothers, we are all too familiar with what other moms are going through. Yet, we hide. We put on a happy face and pretend that we are surviving, making it. We catch another mom's eye in the grocery aisle, and there is a knowing. The glance that is exchanged is almost like that of a soldier in battle. "I get it. You can do this. We are both weary, but we can do this."

The news would paint us as those who engage in

"mommy wars." Petty, shallow, and squabbling over every little detail of how we parent our children. Breast or bottle? Attachment or cry-it-out? Baby-led weaning or cereal at four months? Public school or homeschool? The opportunities for disagreement and division are endless.

But when I meet moms in real life, I don't see that. I see women who want so badly to be told they are okay. That if their child is alive and thriving, they are doing something right. That if they are loving their child the best way they know how, and providing for them in the best way possible, then they are a good enough mom.

Before I had my daughter, I pictured what the perfect mom would look like. I wanted so badly not to "screw her up" or send her into therapy. I read every book, scrolled through every single online forum, read every internet article available from all sides. But the older she got, the more I realized, she doesn't need the perfect mother. She needs me. And I am going to screw her up. Somewhere along the way, I am going to fail her. I already have. I am not going to be the best version of myself. But I can wake up every morning and allow this motherhood journey to shape me, and I can continue to work on my own healing. I can lean on God's grace. And I can pray that I would steward her life well, and that when she takes flight, that I can say I did my very best with what I had at the time.

There is no room for pettiness. There is no room for competition. Because this work, our work, is too important. We can't get caught up in what doesn't matter. Time is too short, things are too hard and too dark for us to not be in this together. The world needs us, and it needs our kids to be healthy and whole. The world needs us to activate our most secret longings and passions to make a difference. The world needs us to sing a redemption song over our kids, over ourselves, over the brokenness, over the hatred, over the despair.

So, here, in this space? I'm invoking the mom code. You are safe here. Your fears, your dark feelings, your frustration, your sadness, your disappointment, they are welcome here. You don't have to pretend it's easy, and you can also gush about how amazing your kids are and how much you love them. Because right here, there is knowing, there is shared experience, and there is grace for you. We are all in the trenches together. We are doing the holy work of shaping the future, and we need each other.

As I write this, my two daughters are having quiet time in their room. I am drinking a thrice warmed-over cup of coffee. And I'm praying that somewhere inside this book, you find freedom. You find a deep sense of not-aloneness. You find yourself again. You see your story in my story, somewhere, and you connect to that little girl who didn't have inhibitions. Who dared to dream. Who made a vow that her life would make a difference, even if you aren't sure anymore what that even means.

Meet me here?

CHAPTER 2

DRINK THE
WILD AIR

———

*The most fundamental vocation is to become
the person that God created you to be.*

Father James Martin

What do you want?

I know, that's a trick question. Let me clarify

What, exactly, do you want?

Does it feel funny to be asked that question? You
haven't had much time to think about that in years now,
am I right? It may border on outrageously selfish for you
to even consider that notion.

But please, consider it. Take a moment and quiet your
mind. What pops into your head? Okay, after the nap and
the shower?

Closer. You're moving in. Yes, that. There it is. A

little hazy still, I know, but keep reading, we are heading somewhere, I promise.

Growing up, it seemed like I was always too much. I asked too many questions, pushed back, and managed to infuriate at least a handful of my teachers. Early on, I got the sense that to make it in the world, I needed to shrink myself somehow—to pull back on the rough edges, soften myself, quiet myself, tone it down.

As I entered adulthood, I also began to believe that my desires were somehow something that I needed to play down, to mistrust, and even to ignore. I was told that I could be anything I wanted to be by my family, but the outside message was clear: there were limits. Sure, I could dream about being president of the United States or running a huge company, or even becoming a "worldchanger," a word so flagrantly tossed around at church youth events, but is that really what God wanted for me? How much of that was vain ambition and a need to be affirmed, to be recognized, approved of? Suddenly figuring out the difference between my ego and "God's calling" on my life became very murky waters.

At the ripe age of twenty-five, I felt a strong urge to leave corporate work and enter the nonprofit sector. I found my first "ministry" job as an administrative assistant at a local organization that worked with pastors and churches in the city. It was a huge time of growth and learning, but after three years, I could see that my ability to grow beyond my current role was limited.

In a leap of faith in 2009, my husband and I made the very reasonable choice to quit all the things and take a month-long road trip out west. It was very Kerouac of us, minus the drugs. I knew I was at a turning point. I needed a sign, something telling me where to go from here. I placed a marker in the road, and said "okay, this has been good so far. But the journey ends (and begins) here. God, please lead the way."

We drove out to the California coast, wandered through giant Redwoods, got desperately lost in an Oregon forest, swam in a crystal-clear mountain lake, and camped out under the stars with the sound of the ocean lulling us to sleep. And when I got back, I knew what I wanted, more than anything in the world.

To write.

Unfortunately, I had underestimated the effects of the 2008 economic crash. There were no jobs to be had, anywhere. I scrapped around with minimal freelancing work, mostly corporate copywriting that paid very little. I went around to every single coffee shop in town and begged for barista work, but no dice. I was unemployed, and we were flat broke.

Everything I had learned and experienced up to that point felt like it added up to a big pile of nothing. It didn't matter. My leap of faith landed me in a dead end, going nowhere. I looked back and wondered what I was thinking. How could I have done something so stupid? Who was I to think I could make a living doing the one thing I loved most? There I went again, being too bold, too brash, dreaming too big.

What I didn't know was that God had placed certain desires in my heart since I was a little girl that would be His gentle whisper of calling in my life. Everything I had experienced with my work—the good, the bad, and the ugly—was pulling me toward something. A calling that would take years to uncover, like a precious stone wrapped in layers and layers of cloth, locked in a chest in the attic. A calling that was ultimately leading me back to myself.

VOCATION (FROM LATIN: VOCÁTIÓ, MEANING "A CALL, SUMMONS")

An occupation to which a person is specially drawn or for which (s)he is suited, trained, or qualified. Though now often used in non-religious contexts, the meanings of the term originated in Christianity.[1]

Originally, the word "vocation" applied to the calling of God on a person's life to join professional clergy. Over the years, vocation has come to apply to every person's work—their specific talents, skills, and purpose in the world.

Understanding our vocation requires one very specific task: paying attention to our holy desires. I can imagine that you may feel, like I have for so long, that on some level your desires are to be ignored and cast aside as selfish or even sinful. Mothers are told that our ultimate task is to give ourselves up, to disappear behind hot stoves, diapers, and piles of laundry. But Jesus himself set the standard by asking the mother of the sons of Zebedee, "what do you want?"[2]

So, I ask again. What do you want?

This time, don't hold back. Go wild. What are the whispers you have heard in between dreaming and waking? When have you felt most alive? When did time seem to pass in an instant? What are the secret longings of your heart, the ones you have never mentioned to anyone for fear of being laughed off as insane? Say it out loud. There are no wrong answers here. Shout it (okay maybe go into the closet first so you don't scare the kids).

My husband and I just finished re-watching the entire Lord of the Rings series, so forgive the bad throwback here, but before I lead you down this beautiful path, I must issue a warning: Your journey will be fraught with peril. There are powers, dark, obscure powers, that right now, as you read these words, are actively at work against you. They have been around since the beginning, and sadly have yet to be destroyed. If only it were as simple as Gandalf waving his wizard staff to make it all go away.

What makes these powers so successful is our blindness to them. As the Apostle Paul wrote, " ... we wrestle not against flesh and blood, but against principalities, against powers, against the rulers of the darkness of this world, against spiritual wickedness in high places (Ephesians 6:12 KJV)". These powers have been at work for ages to convince us that we do not deserve the fullness of what God offers us in this life. They would constantly whisper that true freedom is simply not available to you. That your desires are wrong, that God doesn't care about what is in the deepest parts of your heart. That you must be good, perform, and please others above all else. That God holds you to the highest standard of behavior, but will not hold you when you inevitably break from the weight of it all. This, of course, is all a lie. But we believe it, don't we? It seems to be hardwired into our cells.

I can tell you, right now, this is not God's heart toward you.

Sadly, we are so caught up in the web of deception about who we truly are, that we don't even know what true freedom smells like. We have lived so long inside the stale air of the prison cell that we mistake it for fresh, wild air. But let me assure you that it is not.

God is out there in the open spaces, beckoning us to come. The wild air is out there. The Spirit is bidding us to come and drink.

Let me assure you that no matter what disappointments and disillusionment you have faced, Jesus is cheering you on. During his ministry, He broke social norms by:

Speaking to women, even those who were broken and cast out by society (John 4:10–26

Healing women (Luke 8:43–48, Matthew 8:14–15)

Ministering alongside women (Luke 8:1–3)

Receiving ministry from women (Luke 7:36–50)

His freedom never shackles. It never adds to the burden—it only lightens, lifts, and raises up. Christ's freedom isn't armies marching or guns blazing. It is quiet, still, and small. But don't you ever doubt its ultimate power to unchain you. God wants you to shed the layers of deception, of pleasing, of expectation and simply be. He loves you because He formed you. He sees you and loves you so deeply, that He is willing to chase you down and pursue your heart by whatever means necessary. He wants you to wake up from this dream, this nightmare. He wants you to be whole, healed, and truly free. Walking in the unwavering assurance that you are a Daughter of the Most High. And that your loud, your wild, your weird is beautiful to Him. It's how He designed you, and the worlds needs every bit of it. No more shrinking, no more second-guessing. No more wondering if your desires are truly sanctified. He put them there. He ordains them and calls them holy. He offers you this journey to wholeness and peace—you must simply take the first step. As I mentioned, the road can be dark, and long, and arduous, but I promise it's worth it.

If I could go back ten years and talk to my twenty-seven-year-old self, there are some things I would tell her. I would say that despite what your parents told you, sweet girl, you do not exist in a bubble, and ultimately, the world is not your oyster. You were born into a broken world, and you are a member of its ecology. You cannot divorce yourself from it, and its brokenness is woven into your DNA (and the church).

The world will always be more than willing to provide a predictable playbook for your life. But Christ offers freedom. Wild air. Lift up your head and drink.

The process may take years, and it is a complex

untangling and unmasking. But I ask that you start today. Start to consider the narratives that you are embracing about yourself. Ask God to reveal to you what is true, what is from His heart, and what is not. Ask Him to tell you how He feels about you as His daughter, an expression of His divine creativity. Ask Him to reveal to you the times when you were confronted by earthly beliefs, religious dogma, or dark and sinister lies that sought to diminish your spirit and dishonor your cherished place in the Father's heart. Ask Him to give you new eyes to separate truth from deception.

I believe that whatever our callings are, we cannot neglect them. This does a disservice to God, ourselves, our families, and society. But how do we make sense of it? How do we find some level of "balance" in a season of life that demands so much of our time, our physical abilities, our presence? I believe there are so many women out there who are wrestling with these questions every single day, just like me. I believe there are women out there who simply will not be painted into a cultural box of Stay-At-Home Mom, Work-At-Home-Mom, or anything else. We are all working. We are all called. If a woman is fulfilled completely in her calling as a mother, this must be affirmed and celebrated. Mothering is a sacred, powerful vocation, complete in and of itself. But for those of us who feel called to mothering as well as something else, we must be willing to commit ourselves to a life that serves our dual callings.

Let's pretend together for a moment. Imagine the bills are all paid, the kids are happily playing, the dishes are done, all the laundry is put away, dinner is simmering on the stove, there are no emails to be returned, no calls to make, no appointments to schedule, no one needs you. Not one single person. And, magically, you aren't tired. You have energy. You feel alert; your outlook is good. You feel hopeful, like things matter right now. You don't feel pressured to better yourself in this moment. Any choice you make is perfectly okay. Nothing is expected; everything is good.

What is it that you instinctively choose to do in that moment? What do you turn to? What brings you life? Do you make something? Do you sing a song? Do you dance around the room, or make a cup of tea and sit down with a book? Does your mind immediately flood with ideas for businesses and products, websites, and blog posts? Do you think of all the people you love and wonder how they are doing? Do you go outside and plant something? Do you simply flop down on the couch and lie still? Do you go for a walk? Do you pray or read the Bible? Do you write in your journal?

What happens to your mind in those rare in-between spaces, those moments where you are allowed to wander, to be, to remember that little girl inside you? What does she say to you? What would she whisper if you were quiet enough to listen? Would she show you the mirror you used to dance in front of, or maybe the tree you used to climb? Or maybe the friend who you loved, or the story you wrote in school, or the instrument you played?

What have you done in your life that you have received confirmation for? That others have told you you are amazing at, even if you didn't believe it? What are you doing that causes time to pass quickly when you are doing it? These things matter. Pay attention. These are the ways God whispers to us, giving us glimpses of how we are to spend our time. Don't ignore them.

Remember what it was like to feel so caught up in the moment that nothing else mattered? It's not something that only children can attain. Grown-ups just forget that those moments are even accessible to us anymore. So we turn to things that we know are reliable and available—Netflix, merlot, coffee, scrolling endlessly. Whatever makes it all feel okay. Because growing up is the hardest thing we ever have to do. It isn't for the faint of heart, and if we survive it, it's usually with very little light left to give. But let's fight for the light. Let's hold on to it with all we have, and make sure it doesn't die. Because it is worth it. There is a larger story at work, and we are just a part. We have to listen to that little girl. She has great wisdom and secrets to tell.

Okay, so now that all the cards are on the table and you are fully aware of what you are up against and what lies ahead, I ask you, one last time:

What do you want?

Finding the answer may be the most radical and important thing you ever do.

CHAPTER 3

HAVING IT ALL

...How do you do it all? The answer is this: I don't. Whenever you see me somewhere succeeding in one area of my life, that almost certainly means that I am failing in another area of my life.

Shonda Rhimes

Having it all.

It's a crazy notion isn't it? Who really wants it "all" anyway? "All" just sounds exhausting. But it is exactly what I chased for so long.

I would take new business calls while sitting in the car with my kids in the backseat, just praying they would sleep for a few more minutes so I could finish. I attended conference calls in my closet with the door shut, praying that my daughter would finish her nap so that I could nurse her afterward and not during it. On one particularly memorable day, I remember sitting in my dining room on my third client call, my perfect three-week-old daughter resting happily in her rock n' play. I always tried my best to schedule my calls around her feedings, but that day I wasn't so lucky. Right in the middle of a video call, I saw the look. I heard her unhappy grunts, quickly escalating into muffled cries, and I knew. She wasn't going to last much longer without some milk. So, with all the stealth I could muster, I slowly angled the computer screen upward so only my head was visible. I muted my microphone momentarily, nodded my head vigorously to give the appearance of full conversational engagement, arranged the nursing pillow on my lap, and scooped my daughter into my arms. She latched on, and while she nursed, I went about my business. My client was none the wiser.

This is what it looked like to chase it "all."

Each of us receives different messages about what is expected of us as we enter adulthood. These messages can be overt, but often they are subtle. We take our cues from the choices our parents have made, and eventually either accept or reject them. As I mentioned, my mother always worked. I didn't know any other way, and I didn't feel I was missing out. I assumed that every other kid's life was like mine. If I had asked my mom at the time, I don't think she would have told me she was trying to "have it all." I think she would have told me this was what had to be done.

Being an only child meant that I had an innate sense of being special, simply because I was the one who received all the attention. This, coupled with my type-A personality, gave me a very strong sense that I wanted to do something notable with my life—to leave some sort of legacy. I wanted more than anything to rise above mediocrity. I watched the movie Amadeus in high school and wept bitterly with Antonio Salieri as he begged God to make him great and bargained his entire life to simply have the gift that Mozart had. I couldn't imagine a worse fate.

The stories I would hear in school of people who were changing the world were mostly about men. I knew I wanted to be like them, but could I be a woman and also be great? My parents told me I could, and I had a few females to look to in the 1980s: Mary Lou Retton, Sandra Day O' Connor, and my local church's female worship leader, whom I idolized for her angelic voice. I knew I was a girl, but surely that wouldn't make much of a difference, right?

I never gave a single thought to how motherhood would fit into this grand scheme. Becoming a mother was just something that would happen eventually, and it would have to fit into my plans for greatness. Most of the other moms I observed as a child seemed to live in broken-down minivans, wearing defeated ponytails and puffy pleated shorts, smelling vaguely of dirty diapers and stale Cheerios. They seemed very, very tired. And they had this brooding resentment that seemed to boil over at the most awkward moments. Surely that would not be my fate. I mean, yes, I wanted kids, but the "mom life" package? No thanks. When I had kids, they would simply be absorbed into the soaring narrative of glory and achievement that would be my adult life.

My husband and I were married for eight years before it happened. By this time, everyone in our family and even close friends were wondering if we were ever going to have kids. We enjoyed keeping them guessing. We married young and promised each other that we would enjoy our twenties together, just the two of us. And that is exactly what we did. But then it hit me—the itch. You know. That itch. The one that turns babies from squiggly, weird little creatures who produce various disgusting fluids to creatures that are kind of, well, cute.

Maybe you kind of like them a little. Maybe when they make that face, it's kind of adorable. Ok, really adorable. Wait, what was that? No. This cannot be. Babies are just... too much work. Think about all the trips you still want to take! All the money you still want to earn! All the professional and personal goals you have! Your bucket list! Your husband! What will happen to the marriage? No. This cannot be happening. But it happened. A primal undercurrent took over my brain and said "now is the time. You are powerless against my urges."

I informed my husband that the clock had officially begun ticking. I was not the same woman he married. I had a more than perfunctory interest in babies. I began asking questions. I would walk up to random women in church and ask them point blank, "so what's it like being a mom? Do you like it?" Their answers were generally a mixture of pleasant confusion. Why was I doing research anyway? This wasn't something you really thought about;

it was just something you did. Why ask questions? Well, just diving into something headfirst isn't exactly how I operate. If I was going to do this, I would approach it like everything else in my life. There would be a plan, and we would stick to that plan.

So, the plan was to get pregnant, and get pregnant we did. Ten years of marriage, some fun in the bedroom, one tense moment of peeing on a stick, and then, voila. Two pink lines. (I know for many mothers it is not remotely that simple. I'm only sharing my experience, but I honor everyone's journey to motherhood and recognize that often it is extremely difficult and filled with a great deal of grief, loss, and pain.)

I'm sure you remember that feeling. In one brief moment, you realize you are a mother now. And this doesn't just give you a different outlook on your plans or your dreams for the future. You are actually a body that is housing another body—the first home that this new life will ever know. Your heartbeat is the first sound it will hear. And no matter what happens, you are now stuck with each other.

Suddenly you no longer belong to yourself. Your senses are heightened. Everything becomes a potential threat to the health of your baby. You find yourself dreaming about this child, what it will look like, who it will be, what career it will have, how it will smell. You develop a hyperactive imagination for all the things that could go wrong.

The gravity of those two pink lines is beyond anything you've ever known. In between them is every glowing dream and every dark and terrible fear you've ever dared to entertain. You are transported from a world of goals, checklists, productivity, and achievements to a world of fuzzy plans, unstable expectations, and uncertain outcomes. Nothing is sure, except that you are already starting to like this kid. You don't know what the future holds now. Yesterday, you did. Today, you've got nothing but hope.

As I'm sure you've already guessed, absolutely nothing went as planned for us. We lost our first child at twelve weeks, and I bled so much in the process that I almost lost my own life (we'll get to that wild story in a later chapter). Then my second child, my beautiful daughter, Evangeline, arrived. She wrecked me in the most perfect way. The fierceness of my love for her turned me inside out. This was something I had never known before— feelings so powerful that they could drive me to the end of myself, almost to madness if I let them. Everything that used to matter to me didn't matter anymore. Now I understood.

But as soon as I brought her home, I immediately sensed my pre-mom self tugging at my now-mom self, reminding me of how things used to be. Plans! Greatness! Mary Lou Retton! Remember? It was as though Evie's very existence was a chisel, reshaping my identity. I had no words for it, but I knew. Nothing would ever be the same. I would never be the same. Sweet Evie... she was everything. She was my world. And our little world was beautiful. But part of me grieved for the old Hilary. Some days, when I hadn't slept at all the night before and I wandered around the house in my defeated ponytail, bowl of coffee in hand, smelling of diapers and stale Cheerios, I wondered what had become of me. And then I quickly remembered. I, too, like my mother before me, had some decisions to make. I had to help pay the bills.

I began to feel angry. Why didn't other mothers tell me the truth about how hard this was? Why did those moms at church just smile and nod when I asked them if they liked motherhood? Because this was the absolute hardest thing I'd ever done in my life. Was I crazy, or was every single mom out there just lying? Surely it was one of the two.

Once I became a mother, I found myself firmly situated inside two very competing narratives about what it meant to "have it all." The first came from the women's movement, and the second from the church. Ironically, both of them expected perfection and left very little room for good enough.

Growing up in the 1980s meant growing up in the wake of second-wave feminism. Women were joining the workforce in droves. They were tearing down glass ceilings and pioneering corporate spaces that no woman had ever dared enter. This was wonderful, and it led to so many mothers having more options than ever before. But in all this rush to stake new territory in a man's world, everyone seemed to forget that women were still the ones biologically wired to have babies and feed them, at least for the first few months. What, exactly, were you supposed to do with the children once they were outside of your womb? Because, as Virginia Woolf so eloquently states, "you cannot, it seems, let children run about the streets."[3]

I was one of these children, born in 1981. My mom worked part-time as an educator at the local nursing college inside a respected hospital, and while she was away, I was taken care of in the homes of neighborhood mothers, who offered up their services to care for other women's children so that they, too, could pay the bills.

The women's movement paved the way for women to be accepted in leadership roles at work, but they had to leave their identity as a parent behind. When women went back to work, the expectations for them were consistent with the expectations for every father in the workforce. Sick kid? Sorry, this meeting is very important. Need to get home early for a doctor's appointment? Going to have to reschedule. They had to succeed in a man's world, so they had to act like a man. The old-school corporate model simply does not reward committed parents. To make matters even more difficult, The United States was (and is still) the only developed nation in the world without some form of paid maternity leave.[4] Women with children who must earn an income are forced to make extremely difficult choices.

Integrating personal and professional aspirations proved far more challenging than women had imagined. During the same years that women's careers demanded maximum time investment, their biology demanded that they have children. Their partners did not share the housework and child rearing, so they found themselves with two full-time jobs. The workplace did not evolve to give them the flexibility they needed to fulfill responsibilities at home. Women anticipated none of this. Honestly, I was starting to wonder if all those moms were so quiet because they simply didn't want to burst my fantasy bubble of what I thought motherhood would look like.

The feminist narrative presented through popular culture sells an illusion to young women—the illusion that yes, someday, maybe, you might have kids. But it won't change anything. You will still have a high-powered career, a robust social life, and of course, look fabulous all the time. Having kids is something to "recover from," and quickly. All will be as it was, not to worry. Babies aren't much work. You're really tired for a few weeks, and you live in your pajamas and a ponytail and then, voila! You're back! It's like nothing ever really happened! Be a perfect mom and keep those perfect abs too! Get back "out there" in the workforce and live out that feminine empowered ideal, will you? It's no big deal! And we need not mention the complicated weaving of power, money, and privilege that is involved with this mythical storyline in the first place.

Two women at "the top" offered competing messages from their positions of leadership—the pinnacle of second-wave feminist success. Sheryl Sandberg, Chief Operating Officer of Facebook, author, and billionaire, advises women to "lean in" in her book by the same title,[5] to never quit climbing the ladder, to do what it takes to stay in the corporate game. She places the onus on women to choose their work over their children. No mention, of course, of her billions that allow her to have a full-time staff to care for her household and her children.

Ann Marie Slaughter, a Princeton professor and former director of policy planning for the U.S. State Department, wrote a groundbreaking article in 2012 titled "Why Women Still Can't Have it All."[6] In it she outlines why the old feminist message of having it all simply doesn't add up. She shares her personal story of leaving her high-profile job to be home with her teenage sons. She argues that corporate and cultural institutions must place a higher value on parenting and families to make things truly equal. In her article, she says:

> *Women of my generation have clung to the feminist credo we were raised with, even as our ranks have been steadily thinned by unresolvable tensions between family and career, because we are determined not to drop the flag for the next generation. But when many members of the younger generation have stopped listening, on the grounds that glibly repeating "you can have it all" is simply airbrushing reality, it is time to talk.*[7]

One of my frustrations with so many "business" books for women is that they never make any mention of their kids. It's like they exist in some shadow world, surrounded by nannies and housekeepers. It's as if they aren't even real. These successful corporate women wag their fingers at us, telling us to "lean in," without even recognizing the fact that the "hindrances" they so lament lie within our own bodies. Our ability to bear children is not a curse. The barriers within ourselves are not our mindsets, any more than the mere fact that we have a uterus.

We aren't pulling back because we are afraid. We are pulling back because we are freaking exhausted. Because raising children is a ton of work. We aren't lowering our career expectations per se; we are simply trying to get through the day. We made an entire human being (or two, or three) for crying out loud. We can't just continue on as if that didn't just happen. It's a game-changer. We all don't have the money or the position to afford full-time childcare and household management. Sometimes the numbers simply don't work out. And the double burden is real. We continue to do the majority of the housework and take care of our kids. And we will be for quite some time. And the best you can offer is to tell us "lean in"?

The feminist movement, with all of its successes, ended up ushering women into a new prison of perfectionism, striving, and burnout. Because sadly, the world's vision of success will always leave us empty and yearning for something true and real. The power that you hold is in your ability to respond to God's unique calling for you. To know, without a doubt, that what you are doing is what you are meant to be doing.

The church's message to women regarding motherhood leaves much to be desired as well—that the only role a woman can fill of any importance is that of mother, wife, and homemaker. There is very little understanding of the current economic and social obligations that often require a dual income for survival. Women who must work are questioned for their values and their commitments. Growing up, boys and girls attend the same youth conferences, the same summer camps, and the same VBS programs. They are preached the same message about changing the world. But once women get married and have children, everything shifts. They become a forgotten subset of the church—tucked away in nursing mother's rooms and organizing Tuesday morning mom's groups and playdates. Women in ministry are often assigned to childrens' and womens' ministry roles only, and they are very seldom elevated to the role of Senior Pastor. Mothers, while simultaneously needing so much support and having so much to contribute during this season of life, are usually left to cobble together some semblance of a network in a desperate attempt to build community and keep their sanity intact.

In more traditional church environments, women must not only dutifully carry out their motherhood role, but they must embrace it with their whole being, no complaints. There is simply no conversation about being a working mother, because there is no language for it in the church, and women don't want to talk about it for fear of judgment from other women. Anytime I would turn to a motherhood book in my early parenting days, I would get to the second chapter and close it in disappointment, wondering if there was anything out there for me. I didn't need another book about how to mother like "she" mothered—how to make more creative snacks, or light more candles around the house, or make the perfect pot roast so my kids would truly know I cared about them. I needed someone to tell me that my desire (and economic need) to work wasn't a stain on me, and it wasn't going to ruin my children. That message was nowhere to be found.

The underlying message of everything I read was that because motherhood is the pinnacle of my calling and my life as a woman, it matters more than anything in the world. So I must execute that calling with total perfection to avoid being judged by others—and by God. So much for good enough.

Both the feminist and church narratives landed me right back in the same prison, striving for perfection, exhausted, resentful, and feeling like a total failure. They are both ultimately empty in their expression—one side leaving us feeling truncated and frustrated, as though our humanity and experiences outside of motherhood never mattered, and the other side having us believe our children are simply an inconvenience to be managed as we continue pursuing our dreams. No mother goes one single day without feeling the weight of her choices, one way or another. I had to choose either influence in the workplace or being an awesome mom. It was one or the other, and no matter what I chose, it wouldn't be enough. Who wrote these rules? Because they suck.

Some voices tell us that this motherhood role, this changing the world for one, is all that matters. That this is what we were designed for, made for, created for, and that it is the pinnacle of our role on this earth. Other voices tell us that we must choose to continue changing the world, and we can't allow our children to get in the way of that choice. We are liberated, strong, independent women, and no one can put us in a box.

But both sides leave us wanting.

I am no scientist, but I do know one thing—balance

can't exist without tension and movement.

Newton's first law of motion states: "An object at rest stays at rest and an object in motion stays in motion with the same speed and in the same direction unless acted upon by an unbalanced force." Equilibrium, or balance, means there is no unbalanced force acting upon the object and thus the object maintains its present state of motion.

Notice, there is no presumption that anything is ever fully at rest. Even when you are resting, you are moving, you are breathing. The molecules and cells in your body are acting and being acted upon.

Reaching a state of balance or equilibrium simply means that we maintain our present state of motion. It doesn't mean everything stops. Balance in itself is a fluid state. Have you ever had moments that you wish you could freeze in time so that you could stop and linger just a little while longer? Only, the moment passes and you are left feeling a sense of loss. That's the reality of time—it's fleeting. Change is inevitable.

We may reach a state of equilibrium for a moment, but with life, there is always the guarantee that an unbalanced force is headed our way. We are objects in motion, all the time. Balance, then, is constantly making tiny micro-adjustments to stay upright, to keep our footing, to keep those unbalanced forces (unexpected events) from knocking us over.

No matter what we wish were true, we only have two hands and one mind. We can multitask, for sure, but there are questions about how this affects our brains over time.[8] Our attention is either on one thing or another. A choice to say yes to one thing is a choice to say no to another. No person, woman, or man can be in two places at one time. Omnipresence is unfortunately not a gift granted to us mortals. So we have to choose, and we don't get a do-over. If that's the case, let's be clear about what matters to us, redefine success by our own standards, and drop the myth of "balance".

There will never be a perfect season, a perfect day, or even a perfect hour. But there can be perfect moments. Inside those tiny micro-adjustments, we can be adjusting ourselves. We can shift our perspective. We can work toward a culture and workplace environment that is more supportive of caregivers.[9] We can adjust our expectations and our boundaries and start saying no to things that drain our time and energy. We can see our kids and our work as the gifts that they truly are.

And when we work, when we cook, when we plan, when we comfort, when we read stories, when we commute, when we cuddle, we stay in motion, and we remember that we don't hold up the world. We know who does, and He hold us up as well. That's the secret—God never asked us to live "balanced" lives. He asked us to follow Him. To be with Him. Even in the messiness and the busyness. And that makes everything easier.

Perhaps you have sensed these competing narratives in your life, and neither of them work for you. Maybe you haven't been able to put words to it, but you have found that you don't necessarily fit anywhere, really. That ever since you had children, you seem to be floating in a strange in-between place. I'm here to tell you that you are not alone.

Maybe our definition of "having it all" has been skewed from the start, and we need to reconsider what it means to be called by God. Not forced into choices because of pressure from any outside force or driven by a sense of obligation or fear, but responding to the specific call of God on our lives, whatever it may be, with no apologies and no excuses. You don't have to neglect your family to be successful, and you don't have to feel guilty for needing to work, or for wanting to. This is something we can live out right now, bringing it into existence as we mother, work, live, and earn. We are declaring that there doesn't have to be a dichotomy. That everything we are, and all that we do, can honor God. That good enough looks messy, but it's still beautiful. The fullness of who we are is made more complete by mothering our precious children and by pursuing our dual callings. God is big enough to hold it all. The labels are handcuffs that we don't have to wear anymore. Our decisions are our own, and we don't have to apologize for them. God is not disappointed in you. He is so very, very proud of you. There is abundance in following your calling. There is room for tension and tightrope walking. He will hold you steady.

We are all walking different paths, and God is present, always speaking, and always loving us along each one. Maybe having it all doesn't look like what we think it does. Maybe making a dent in the world and being "great" looks different for every woman. Maybe there is more open space for a myriad of choices and callings and passions than we ever knew.

Maybe, just maybe, God is whispering something new and beautiful, and we need to listen and respond.

CHAPTER 4

BIG T, LITTLE T, WHAT BEGINS WITH T?

———

The right way to wholeness is made up of fateful detours and wrong turnings.

Carl Jung

When my girls were smaller, we loved to read Dr. Seuss's ABC book. Each letter in the alphabet was presented as a big letter and a little letter: "BIG A, little a, what begins with A? Aunt Annie's Alligator. A...a...A." I probably read that book thousands of times, and it occurred to me that we can apply big and little letters to many aspects of life. For me, that was true when it came to trauma. I learned about trauma by navigating my own, and it was here that I discovered both "Big T" trauma and "little t" trauma existed in everyone's life on some level. Big T trauma gets much more attention, but little t can do some serious damage as well. Big T trauma swept into my life at age thirty, and it was related to childbirth. I know so many women who have experienced trauma around childbirth, even when the ultimate outcomes were positive, and "healthy mom, healthy baby" was achieved from a medical and physiological standpoint. However, so many mothers and would-be mothers suffer in silence from grief, loss, and trauma, and this informs so many of the choices that we make once our precious babies do arrive in our arms, earthside.

My experience with pregnancy loss changed me forever. It changed how I view the children I'm now parenting, how I view my body, and how I view my life. If you have ever experienced this, you know that it is a club no one ever wants to join, but once it happens, you are ushered in the back door with quiet support and love. Women come out of the woodwork to tell you that they too have suffered this pain. You marvel at how many women you know who carry this grief but who had never shared it with you before. It's often swept under the rug, working itself out in silence. Some types of suffering in this world are given a stamp, a banner, a flag to wave, a way to identify the pain and anguish. Some are not. Pregnancy loss is one of those sufferings—the kind that leaves you not only feeling lost and hopeless but confused and isolated. Who am I in light of this? Who can I turn to? Where do I go from here?

If you have had the experience of being welcomed into this most unfortunate club, I applaud you for your courage.

This is my story.

At twelve weeks pregnant, my husband and I received the heartbreaking news that the baby I had been carrying for twelve weeks stopped growing at six. The baby hadn't made it past six weeks, which means I spent six weeks dreaming about a baby inside of me, a life inside of me, that was already gone. I often think about the cruelty of that timing. I was thirty years old, and in early January, when winter in the South is cold and bleak, I began to bleed. I knew something was wrong, so we went in for an ultrasound. The doctor told us that the baby had stopped growing. No explanation. Just a diagnosis: "embryonic demise." I'll never forget seeing those words on the paper that my midwife handed to me. I felt numb all over. It seemed as though all the emotions I had felt— the excitement, the love, the growing bond with this little child inside of me—had simply been a cruel joke.

The doctor offered a vague apology, but I couldn't hear anything. His lips were moving but no sound was coming out. I was undone. I crumpled onto the floor in the hallway of the doctor's office, sobbing and heaving uncontrollably. The next day I began to bleed even more, as I had been told would happen. I opted to allow the miscarriage to happen on its own, and I was sent home with a prescription for a painkiller. I gave birth to my baby in our bathroom, barely recognizable as a fetus, but still, my precious baby. My husband and I said some parting words and flushed it down the toilet. What else could we have done? I didn't know at the time. Maybe now, looking back we could have buried that tiny, precious body in the ground. But at the time I couldn't stand to prolong the goodbye. It had already felt like a thousand years waiting for it to come out of my body. That's when the real bleeding began. I thought this was completely normal, but by evening I was standing in my bathtub, bleeding grapefruit-sized blood clots. My bathroom looked like a scene from the movie Carrie. I knelt down in the bathtub, scrubbing the blood away, but I couldn't keep up. There was too much. I began to feel lightheaded and wondered if maybe this was too much blood. I called my father-in-law, who was a doctor, to tell him what was going on. He said to go to the hospital immediately. I hung up the phone, shoved some pads into my pants to try and keep the blood from leaking all over my clothes and car, and quickly left the house.

As I walked down the front steps to the sidewalk, my legs stopped working and my vision began to go black. I thought to myself "this is it. I'm dying". Then I passed out, face down on the sidewalk. My husband carried me to the car and sped to the emergency room. I came to in the backseat, at ninety miles an hour on I-65. I immediately began screaming in tongues, a language I couldn't understand, but one I had received as a young girl at church camp. I yelled and prayed, battling whatever was trying to take my life away that night, saying, "No! Not tonight!" I was rushed into the emergency room and hooked up to monitor after monitor. The remaining twenty-four hours was a blur of screening rooms, blood draws, beeping machines, and eventually an emergency D&C in the early hours of the next morning. I shifted in and out of consciousness, but once I fully woke up, the bleeding had stopped. Apparently, my uterus was oddly shaped, and it had been hanging on to a remnant of my child that it was trying to flush. My body didn't want to let go.

I laugh now at the doctors who told me I would be "back to normal" after two weeks. What is "normal" after you've lost a child? And do you even want to get back there in the first place? I have always been one who likes to find the silver lining in every situation, tying things up with a pretty bow. I did this the best I could, but the day that I got home from the hospital I knew I would never be the same.

Someone from my workplace sent a sympathy card to my home, and when I crawled into bed after returning home, it was sitting on my bedside table. The card had a picture of Jesus on the front, holding a lamb in his arms. Next to the lamb I wrote my name in pen. I was so unbelievably sad, raw, depleted, and broken, and I knew only Jesus could hold me. I couldn't put a silver lining on this, not today. I just needed to be held. I looked at that card every morning and asked Jesus to hold me in my grief and sorrow. And He did.

I took a leave of absence from my job, took a semester off of graduate school, and spent the following weeks on my couch with my dog, watching 30 Rock and sleeping. I had no energy to do anything. My arms ached with longing to hold my baby. I felt exhausted and panicked all at once. A few weeks after being released from the hospital, I found myself back in the emergency room due to chest pains, which turned out to be a panic attack. I spent hours on the phone with my midwife, who prescribed anything that she thought could bring me some relief, but some of the medication left awful side effects. I knew that my mental state was deteriorating, so I agreed to go on anti-depressants.

As I began to process this event in the following months and connect with more women, I realized that I had inadvertently joined a new club—the Pregnancy Loss Club. The thing about this club is that as an expectant mother, you barely know it exists, or if you do, you would rather not think about it. And only once you are initiated are you grateful it exists at all so you don't have to go through this alone.

Women just simply don't talk about pregnancy loss as often as they should. Once I had experienced it, women began confiding in me that they, too, had suffered a miscarriage, stillbirth, or pregnancy loss of some kind. I couldn't believe it. Some of these women I had known most of my life, and I had no idea the pain and grief they had endured until I endured it myself.

I wondered if this was somehow like the motherhood club—no one tells you the truth about it until you join. Why do we do this? Why do we sweep the most profound and deeply impactful events under the rug? Why do we grin and bear it? I realize that social media has allowed women to be more open with their stories, and I am grateful for that. But what about the real-life women who you know? Do you know if they suffered a loss? Do you know what they went through to bring their children into the world? These are the stories we must tell each other, face to face, listening with our hearts and our ears and not just reading about it on a screen. These stories matter because they remind us that we are not alone.

The grief and pain of losing an unborn child, whether it is at twelve weeks or forty, is one of the heaviest experiences you can endure in this life. The hope, the anticipation, the dreams that are wrapped up in those two pink lines are enough to consume your entire being. You don't know the first time around that there is a chance you could lose the child, and even if you did know that statistics or had heard stories, you don't want to give yourself space to think about it. The tug of war between hope and fear pulls more strongly in the direction of hope, and that makes any loss all the more difficult. I constantly imagined all I had hoped this baby would become, all the memories we would make together, and how this life and our family would be forever changed because of this tiny human's existence. And in one fell swoop, one ultrasound, one doctor's verdict, it was all taken away. Hope instantly fades into the distance and your new reality is emptiness. Empty arms that long to hold your child, now dangling, heavy, throbbing. It's as if your arms are actually grieving, your chest feeling the weight of where your baby would have laid. It's all too much to bear. But you bear it anyway, pushing through the days, the sleepless and agitated nights. Taking deep breaths when you think the sadness might steal your breath for good. Trying to find joy in the small moments and remind yourself that this isn't the end.

After this Big T Trauma, I set my sights on healing. And like anything else I pursued in life, this would be no different. I would take it head on, set goals, tackle it piece by piece until I felt well enough to try to conceive again. This was the beginning of my immersion into deeper forms of alternative medicine, although I had been exposed to things like chiropractic care and supplements prior to this. But I was desperate to heal, desperate to move on and have a real live baby in my arms. I knew that in my current state there was no way I could support a baby in my body. I knew I had work to do. So I rolled up my sleeves and got to work.

At the time I was still taking anti-depressants and anti-anxiety medication to keep me functional, and I didn't even realize what a gift they were to me. I had a history of anxiety and panic that dated back to my childhood, and I had taken Paxil in college right after I got married. Big life transitions seemed to trigger these situations in me, and as much as I felt I had failed in some way, I knew that I needed them. There is still so much stigma around this, but when you are suffering, you have to do what it takes to function. You have to get through the day. And so I stayed on the meds, but I made a game plan to get off them whenever I was ready.

One of the things that I did when I first began to grieve (besides cry a lot) was to write. I discovered through the process of grieving that suffering births creativity. It goes back as far as David and the Psalms. The trials we face give rise to the heights of our creative ability. Expressing our grief, whether through song, art, or the written word, is woven throughout human history. When I first found out that I was pregnant, I began a journal to the "Bean," as I called it. The following poem is the last entry I wrote the day after we found out. I was outside with our dog, and I heard a bird chirping. It triggered something inside of me, and I went upstairs and wrote this short poem.

I'LL SEE YOU IN THE SPRING

Can you hear the sparrow sing? Do you know its tone, its ring?

When the leaves are off their branches, can you see them in the breeze?

Can you see the sun, its light? Its rays stretched out in warm delight?

Can you feel the softest wind as it blows through here and back again?

I'll see you in the spring, my child. I'll see you in the spring.

When all is new, the world is green, and all is right that's ever been.

Can you hear my whispering voice? Do you know its tone, its ring?

Can you feel my heart break too, at the very thought of you?

I'll see you in the spring, my child. I'll see you in the spring.

When all is new, the world is green, and all is right that's ever been.

Another way that I worked through the grieving process was to create a video montage. It was a montage of us and all our loved ones, family and friends, who would have been a part of our baby's life. It reminds me of all the great times we've had with those people and how dear they are to me. It was definitely something that helped me "memorialize" my baby and bring some closure.

The other modalities I used were talk therapy, acupuncture, and supplementation. My first plan was to process all the grief and trauma that had taken place through this incident, and, of course, this took time—a great deal of time. The first therapy I utilized was EMDR or Eye Movement Desensitization and Reprocessing. It is a treatment that allows your mind to reprocess traumatizing events, thereby "training" your brain to process these negative memories in a new way. For example, when I think about some of the traumatic things that happened, such as the bleeding or passing out, this therapy helped me to identify the triggers and not be overtaken by panic and negative emotions.

My therapist taught me that with Big T traumas, your mind and body get stuck in that moment. When I passed out, it didn't matter that I wasn't actually dying. What mattered is that my brain believed that I was dying. And that sense of helplessness, being trapped in a situation you can't escape, is trauma at its most basic level. The hospital scene wasn't any less gruesome than the bathroom scene at home. I was placed in a triage room with a bedpan to catch the grapefruit sized blood clots that continued to be expelled from my body. The nurses couldn't seem to change the bedpan fast enough. The heart monitor I was attached too would aggressively beep when my heart rate would go above 100 beats per minute, which was the entirety of my time in triage. To this day it is difficult for me to hear hospital monitors, even though I have healed this particular trauma as deeply as possible. Going through EMDR was a difficult process. It left me exhausted, but feeling as though I was rewiring my brain somehow. That I was taking this horrific experience and not continuing to re-experience it every single day. That on some fundamental level, I was healing.

The next approach I tried was acupuncture. A friend of mine at the time was a naturopath, and after recommending several supplements to me, she told me about an acupuncturist she knew. I was ready to try anything at that point, so I made an appointment. I went several times, but I did not expect to have such a profound experience. I don't know much about Chinese medicine, except that it is based on the theory that our life force runs through certain meridians inside of our body. When you place needles at specific meridian points, it can activate life force, or Qi, to the organs that run along those meridians, thereby promoting healing and balance.

I didn't bargain for a completely mind-blowing spiritual experience during one of my sessions one day. Mind you, I grew up Pentecostal. As in, hand raising, flag waving, speaking in tongues, and falling out Pentecostal. I am no stranger to the supernatural, and I have seen and personally experienced my fair share of "charismatic" moments throughout my life. But what I experienced one day while lying on the table was something I never imagined was possible.

For some reason every time I would receive an acupuncture treatment, it was like someone had given me a sleeping pill. I would fall into a deep sleep state within just a few minutes of beginning the session. I believe this has something to do with the sympathetic nervous system, but I'm honestly not sure. Whatever the reason, there I was lying on the table, sleeping. Suddenly I felt a warm light come over me. The glow of it felt like every joyful emotion I've ever had, bathing me in this beautiful light. I looked up and there was my child, my baby, my son. My beloved grandmother was holding him. My son began to speak to me, surrounded by this warm light that I could have basked in forever. He said, "Mommy, I'm okay. I'm safe now. I'm healthy and strong. You don't have to worry about me. Grandma met me here and she is taking great care of me. We can't wait for you to join us someday."

Tears began streaming down my cheeks as I slept. I didn't want to leave this place, whatever it was. I couldn't believe I was given such a beautiful gift—the gift of knowing my son was okay. That he was alive and could see into my future even when I couldn't. That someday I would see him again. This was too much for me to process.

As I awoke to the quiet room, I was in shock. What had just happened? How could this be? I had never experienced anything like this in my entire life, and I had seen some crazy things. But at the same time, I felt this deep longing to be back there, basking in the light. I would have given anything for just one more moment there. But I knew what I had been given was a gift, a glimpse. I don't know why and I don't know how, but recognizing it as a gift was the only way I could see it.

As I worked through the various methods and approaches of the grieving process, I found healing, but this took several years. I have always been proactive in my pursuit of growth and healing, and although I approached this as a challenge to be overcome, I realize now that everything I did was guided and supported by God. The practitioners I was led to work with, the timing of the treatments and therapies, and the way things unfolded in my healing process were all as they should have been. So often I don't trust that, and I try to heal myself too quickly. But when I am fully connected, I know and remember that I am being guided, and it is not up to me to push and cajole and strive, but simply to receive.

Life is both fragile and it is resilient. I like to use the term "fragilient". I will never again take for granted the fact that a child can be conceived, grow, and be born healthy. It is an utter miracle that everything works so perfectly as to make this happen. No one's life is a waste. If you were born, God meant for you to be. I used to be so confident in my body's ability to achieve things for which I took complete credit. Proverbs 9:10 says, "the fear of the Lord is the beginning of wisdom," but I never truly understood what that verse meant. I am grateful that now I can grasp its meaning and stand in complete awe and reverence of the God who gives and who takes away.

I took pride in being healthy and fit. And while there

is nothing wrong with striving to be healthy, I now have a new understanding of who is in charge of my body. I can't achieve a successful pregnancy just because I avoid bad foods and exercise. God is in control of everything that happens to me, good or bad. And my attitude should be one of thankfulness for each day that I get to wake up and feel great. Sometimes God grants us a severe mercy, we just have to be able to see it. A whole new sense of perspective came from that experience. For some people it may have just seemed like one crappy hand after another, but I have to believe that God was trying to open my eyes and help me see how He was working in the situation. It is in the most scary and awful moments in life that we discover whether or not our faith is truly real to us.

When I needed God, He was there. He comforted me when I was sick, and He gave me peace when I was scared. I made a decision that I was going to believe that God is good, no matter what my circumstances told me. Because that is the truth. And without it, I don't know what I would do. Throughout the ordeal, I was surrounded by the love of family and friends and the prayers of the saints. I felt the healing prayers of friends in my physical body and was nourished by the comforting words and tears of those who grieved with me. I was fed by the many hot meals that were brought to my home. I learned how to receive from others. I had conversations with my parents that brought us closer, and witnessed my husband rise to the occasion as an incredible caregiver.

I know that pregnancy loss is something so many women experience, but like any experience of loss or grief, it reminds us of our humanity. For so many years women hid these losses, kept them private, and even felt a sense of shame. I can't tell you how many times I wondered, "*did I do something to cause this? Did I eat something wrong or exert myself too much?*" An even deeper sense of shame and guilt can take root when you believe your genes may be defective, that something is wrong with you on a cellular level. That your body may not be able sustain life. This shame runs deep and is very hard to shake.

No one told me that the path to healing was long and winding, with many twists and turns. It has been eleven years since my loss. I now have healthy nine-year-old and six-year-old daughters. They are full of life and energy, and they light up my life every single day. I always look at them and remember that they are gifts, they are miracles, that their very existence is a testament to God's love, creativity, and faithfulness. There are days that I take them for granted, of course. But I am always working to remember how precious their lives are and the magnitude of what I've been given in this life. Sometimes you have a deeper appreciation for what has been given when you have endured suffering and loss. The wound is where the light enters.

CHAPTER 5

BIRTH PLANS & OTHER USELESS DOCUMENTS

———

It moves one's heart to think:
nine months before I was born,
there was a woman who loved me deeply.
She did not know what I was going to be like,
but she loved me
because she carried me in her womb.
And when she gave me birth,
she took me in her arms
because her love was not just beginning—
she conceived it along with me.

Oscar Romero, "The Violence of Love"

I know for some, their life experiences only tend to reinforce their dearly held beliefs. Unfortunately (or fortunately) for me, this has never been the case. At every turn, my circumstances have forced me to stare my own judgment calls in the face and realize they were complete horse poo. Dogma can only remain dogma until experience proves otherwise.

In this case, this experience came in the form of birthing my first daughter. I had recovered from my miscarriage enough that my husband and I felt comfortable beginning to try again for another child, and the pregnancy was uneventful. It followed the standard pattern, and I was grateful for this, considering my previous experience. I did not take this life inside of me for granted one bit, but I can't say that I necessarily enjoyed being pregnant. Motherhood offers itself to us in the form of endless contradictions and extremes, and this was the first one I encountered. I could be so in love with this life inside of me, so grateful for the miracle that was unfolding in my womb, while also being somewhat miserable as a pregnant lady. The early months of extreme nausea (which I was consciously thankful for because it served as a reminder that this baby was growing and thriving), cravings and aversions, the constant peeing, the hormone spikes that made me completely nuts, and the end of the pregnancy when I was the size of a Thanksgiving Day parade float—all of the physical frustrations mixed with the wonder and excitement of it all were out of this world.

There are many things that I didn't know about pregnancy, but one that came as the biggest surprise to me is that the due date truly means nothing. This date that you hang your every hope upon can come and go without so much as a whimper. It can become just another day, and that is a strange feeling. Exactly one week before my due date, I began having what's known as "prodromal labor." I had very mild contractions for twenty-four hours that felt like the beginning of labor, but it never progressed. Being awakened in the middle of the night with pain made it hard to sleep—that first night I simply sat in anticipation and excitement. I took the next few days off work to relax and wrap my head around what was happening. There is nothing more frustrating than being in pain and then being told it is "false labor." Nothing about it feels false. My doula told me to take a few Benadryl and get as much sleep as possible, that this was the beginning and I would need my rest. Two days later Matt and I did some of the typical "helpful" activities to bring on labor. Those included, among the obvious, eggplant parmesan, brisk mall walking, and acupuncture. I just knew we could help things along!

The following Friday evening, one day after the due date, I began to have pains again. We were watching Star Wars with some friends (yes, you read that correctly), and I decided that this was definitely it. I went to take a long shower and thought for sure I would be in full-on labor within the next few hours. Instead, I had mildly painful contractions all night and into the next morning. By the following day I was so tired and frustrated. My doula told me to take another Benadryl and a nap, but I couldn't sleep. I called my best friend and asked her if we could go get some frozen yogurt, and she took me to get a pedicure as well. We asked the gentleman who was giving my pedicure to press really hard on the pressure points that induced labor. He must have done something right.

Matt came home later that evening, and I distinctly

remember telling him that I was dreading the possibility of going into labor that night because I was so exhausted. Well, about five minutes later I did just that. I remembered that my doula had told me, "you will know when it's the real thing." Now I understood what she meant. This was much more painful than my previous contractions. I looked at Matt and told him it was finally time. At this point, I think we were both so doubtful that it was actually happening that we didn't really accept it until about an hour later when my contractions were coming much closer together. So, my journey into natural labor began on Saturday, December 3, 2011, two days after my due date, at nine o'clock in the evening.

We called our doula and let her know the "real thing" was going down, and she told me to run a hot bath, light some candles, and labor in the tub at home. So I did, and it was amazing. It's incredible how relaxing the hot water is and how much easier it is to labor. I stayed there for a few hours and then got out to labor on the birth ball. At this point it was around one o'clock in the morning. My best friend came over and blow-dried my hair while I labored in bed, and Matt buzzed about getting our bags ready for the hospital. My doula arrived soon after, and we decided to head to the hospital at around one-thirty in the morning.

I labored in the back seat on the birth ball on the way to the hospital and in the parking lot. Thankfully there was no traffic, and we actually ended up being the only people in labor and delivery that night. At this point, my contractions were pretty overwhelming. I went from moaning and wailing to staying completely silent and just letting the pain wash over me. I was amazed that I was handling it so well. But I remembered what I had learned about focusing on one contraction at a time, and my doula counted down the seconds until it was over. Matt was my number one cheerleader.

When we arrived at the hospital, they checked me, and I was dilated nine centimeters. I couldn't believe it! I was so elated that I had made it that far already and assumed that I would be pushing within the next few hours. We checked in to the labor and delivery suite, and I continued to labor on the birth ball for a while. I would hang on to Matt and go through a contraction, and he would hold me up with his arms. He was my rock, as usual.

I decided to get in the shower after a while, and labor under the hot water again. This helped with the pain, but by this time I was reaching the point of complete exhaustion. I was falling asleep on the shower floor in between contractions. My doula told me that the number one enemy of natural labor isn't pain but exhaustion, and not having sleep going into the process, this was certainly true for me. When I was in the shower, I remember having this sinking feeling that something just wasn't right. Things weren't progressing like they should have been. An on-call doctor (not my regular doc, but wonderful nonetheless) broke my water and then checked me a few hours later. I was still at nine centimeters, and Evie was still at negative two station, not descending at all. Her head was slightly sideways and continued to hit against my cervix without being able to move into the birth canal.

By seven o'clock the following morning, the nurses decided to place me in the "pretzel" position to see if that would help move Evie into the right space to descend. This made the pain completely unbearable. At this point I was beyond exhausted, and I simply couldn't stand it anymore. I begged for the epidural! I remember telling the anesthesiologist that if he didn't get the medication in me before the next contraction, he would be getting a slap in the face. To my surprise, my doctor actually tried to talk me out of it. Despite all of my preconceived notions about doctors pushing drugs, my experience was just the opposite. She looked me in the eye and said, "remember your birth plan. I just don't want you to do anything you will regret later." But at that point, I had simply had enough.

I must say, the epidural was quite lovely. Not only could I finally relax, but that was the most comfortable I had been not just in labor, but during my entire pregnancy! We all rested for about three hours as my contractions continued, and the staff monitored the baby's progress.

Unfortunately, by noon that day, nothing had changed. I was still at nine centimeters, and Evie hadn't budged. At this point they decided to give me Pitocin to strengthen my contractions and see if that would help move things along. The only thing it did was stress her out and make her heart rate go haywire. We held out as long as we could. I didn't want to think that I might end up in what in my mind was a worst-case scenario: a Caesarean Section. The doctor was so patient, and she told us that the baby would need to come out eventually, but that she wasn't in danger, and we could take our time to process the situation.

Once it hit me, I began to cry. Hard. I couldn't believe that after all this we had no other option. That nothing had changed. Matt and I had a moment alone. We cried together. It was a really beautiful moment. I asked him if he was disappointed in me and if he thought I should have tried harder. I asked him if I had made the right decisions. Through tears, he told me that I was amazing and he was so proud of me. Those words wouldn't have meant the same thing to me if I had achieved the smooth natural delivery that we had hoped for.

So on the afternoon of Sunday, December 4, I was wheeled into the operating room. At this point, I just wanted to meet my daughter. Matt met me in the room. I wasn't scared. I had disassociated myself from what was actually happening and was just focused on Evie. I was fully awake and alert the whole time. Matt was right by my side. We wrote a song for her called "Face to Face" and he played it on his phone during the procedure and the moment she was born. It was absolutely beautiful. Needless to say, we were a mess of tears. I had been opened up and my child had been removed from my body and placed on my chest, and it was the most other-worldly moment of my entire life. I never imagined the amount of love I could have for another human being.

The history of childbirth throughout the world is fraught with drama and the medical establishment asserting its knowledge into what once was a primarily female enterprise. The medicalization of birth and the development of pregnancy into a condition to be monitored rather than a natural event have shifted the landscape forever. Yes, it has saved many lives in the process, but many lives have been sacrificed on that altar as well. What I do know is that finding a place to land in the complex, historical, social, cultural, and personal history around birth is hard. The fear of birth is hardwired into us from day one. We are taught that this experience is something that will be the most painful thing we ever endure, and that it is risky, so very risky. We hear about the maternal mortality rate rising steadily in America while in other countries it continues to decline, and we shiver with fear. We watch The Business of Being Born and swear that we will have a natural birth at home.

This is exactly what I did. I have always been open to alternative medicine, probably because I always had weird issues that typical MDs couldn't seem to put their finger on. So I watched Ricki Lake have her baby in a tub, I read Ina May Gaskin, and I decided that I was going to take my birth back. I was going to do this naturally, and I was going to wear that badge with pride.

I wrote out a two-page birth plan and submitted it to my doctor. I was determined not to be overtaken by fear during labor and make a decision I would later regret. I had every contingency planned for. Nothing could possibly happen that could throw this plan out of whack. But then, my baby just wouldn't come out. For twenty-four hours, she wouldn't descend. And that was that. Birth plan, out the window.

Dr. John Kabat-Zinn wrote in his book Full Catastrophe Living: Using the Wisdom of Your Body and Mind to Face Stress, Pain, and Illness, "Since the time of Descartes in the seventeenth century, Western scientific thinking has divided the intrinsic wholeness of being into separate, essential non-interacting domains of soma (body) and psyche (mind)."[10] Dr. Kabat-Zinn argues against this belief, and, like him, I believe the mind, body and spirit are intrinsic, whole, one. Messy and layered, yes, but ultimately one. It was hard to prove that when my own body didn't align with my will. The body has a wisdom that we sometimes cannot know. We are convinced by experts that we don't know what is best for our own offspring—that we should ignore the primal urges, submit ourselves to the dualistic model, and use our higher cognitive thinking during birth. But our lizard brains know what to do—they always have. We just need to listen and listen well. I heard that so much, and I repeated that mantra over and over before having my baby. We are told to trust our bodies, but I have to be honest with you, I don't think I was in a position to do that at the time.

Looking back, I realize that I still had layers of personal trauma to wade through, and a disconnection from myself that I wasn't even aware of when I gave birth to my daughter. My overriding instinct was fear and anxiety. Although I am proud of myself for getting to nine centimeters dilation on my own, for whatever reason, my child could not exit my womb on her own. Doctors used the term "asynclitic" which simply means my daughter's head was turned the wrong way. Maybe my uterus was still oddly shaped? Who knows. Either way, my body had betrayed me again. It had not done the most primal, natural thing that women have been doing for centuries—birthed a healthy baby vaginally. This betrayal of one's own body against one's own mind and will causes intense feelings of grief and confusion.

Once again, the contradictions of motherhood surfaced. I wanted someone to blame for this. Maybe if the doctors hadn't given me the epidural? Maybe if I had just held out a little longer? Did I not have what it took? Who could I be angry with? Whose fault was this? All of these questions plagued me even while I was completely over the moon with my beautiful daughter and just so happy she was in my arms. Now, years later, we will often lie in her bed at night and she will ask me how she was born. And even though I'm honest with her about the pain and the surgery, I will tell her I would do it all over again, a million times, just to have her.

Even knowing that, the grief lingers. The loss of the experience you dreamed you would have. The birth that you had been picturing, planning for, imagining for months wasn't to be. I think this happens to so many women in so many ways, big and small, during the birth process that it's hard to fathom. Even if your birth goes perfectly as planned, there is always the sheer shock of giving birth at all that is enough to send you reeling for months and even years.

I understand the rage against doctors who force unnecessary Ceasarean Sections, and I know the pain of feeling like you were taken advantage of in one of the most vulnerable and scary moments in your life. It is real, and it is an injustice. But in our crusade to strengthen women in childbirth, we have ostracized and shamed the women who were not able to deliver their babies in the most natural of ways. And this itself is an injustice. As women, we should celebrate all life, no matter how it enters the world. We should seek to be informed, empowered, and educated about birth—and not only how transformative it is, but how dangerous it can be.

So often in natural childbirth, we are told to "trust the birthing process." I'm sorry, but I don't understand this. I don't trust the birthing process. It has killed millions of women throughout the centuries. I trust my own instincts to know what is best for me and my baby, and I trust the care of those whom I have invited in to help me in the process, be that my spouse, my midwife, my doctors, and those who care deeply about the outcome of my birth. I trust the wisdom of God—it has brought me through two births that didn't exactly follow my birth plan, but the end result was still just as sweet.

The pressure to be the perfect mother starts long before a baby exits the womb. Not only must you deliver a healthy, perfectly formed, adorable human being and then promptly dress it in the cutest outfit and share your smiling "I did it!" picture on social media, but you also have to bring it into the world in just the right way. If you don't, you risk starting out your motherhood journey at a deficit. This is completely insane. So often it seems like this is just one more way for us to compete for some intangible motherhood prize and compare ourselves to each other to see how we measure up. We have to begin finding good enough even before our babies are born. Some of us must learn the hard way.

Birth is powerful. It is one of the most intense spiritual and physical experiences we will ever have in this life. But we rob it of its power when we reduce it to checklists and comparisons. The numinous—the holy and mysterious—is lingering inside of all our birth stories. But when we demystify pregnancy and birth, we remove its power. When we whitewash it and gloss over the hard stuff, we rob it of its redemptive potential. Talking about the hard stuff doesn't call for shame. It infuses beauty and power back into the experience. Hard things shape us. We don't have to pretend it was perfect for it to have been good. Sometimes the good is equal parts magnificent and terrible. Sometimes the good is both holy and mysterious. And in this holy and mysterious act of giving life to someone else, we find ourselves anew. We can see the beauty in the imperfection and unexpected, and we can call all of it good.

CHAPTER 6

MUNDANE & INSANE BEAUTY – A FEW ESSAYS ON MOTHERING IN THE MESS

What would happen if one
woman told the truth about her life?
The world would split open.

Muriel Rukeyser, "Käthe Kollwitz"

Once Evie was born, everything shifted for me. It was like nothing else mattered anymore. I looked into her eyes and everything I ever wanted in life changed.

My universal became very small—about the size of my newborn baby. Her smallest need dictated the rhythm of my days, and my "world changer" mindset shrunk down to the world of one.

Before I realized what was happening, my life became a textbook in Mundanity 101. Wake up. Feed her. Change her. Shower, if I was lucky. Make coffee. Make breakfast. Clean up breakfast. Play with her. Put her down for a nap. Try to figure out what to do with the one to two hours I might have to myself. Spend most of it just sitting on the couch eating something unhealthy. Feed her. Change her. Fix lunch. Clean up from lunch. Put her down for her afternoon nap. Rock her, nurse her, rock some more, soothe her, sneak out of her room. Fix dinner. Clean up after dinner. Bathe her. And finally, put her down for the night—or until she woke up for the next feeding.

Having young children is a practice in the mundane.

MUNDANE

humdrum, dull, boring, tedious, monotonous, tiresome, wearisome, unexciting, uninteresting, uninvolving, uneventful, unremarkable, repetitive, repetitious, routine, ordinary, everyday

Going on an outing or having a playdate became a way to maintain my sanity. Even a doctor's appointment was something to look forward to. Going to the grocery store alone felt like an all-inclusive package to an island resort.

I would wonder how much attention she needed from me. When it was her playtime, did she need me to be playing with her directly the entire time? Or could I work on something while she was playing on her own?

If I played with her too much, would that make her entitled and bratty? If I didn't play with her enough or give her enough, would she feel unloved and be psychologically damaged?

The tension between the demands of my former productivity, my perfectionism, my expectations of myself, and the reality of parenting a baby was thick. So thick, you could cut it with a plastic kiddy spoon. Every single day was a practice in being torn. I still had dreams of my own. And looking into her eyes didn't make me forget those dreams; it made them much clearer. I wanted to continue pursuing my passions and my work, but I wanted to pursue her too. I felt guilty when I didn't spend enough time with her, and I felt resentful when I didn't get to work on my life.

I loved her so much it hurt. But her babyness was consuming. I forced myself to be over-productive during naps, getting as much done as possible when I had the energy. I told myself that I could be just as productive as the next person if I played my cards right. I needed to figure out life hacks, to use every tool at my disposal to maximize my time with her and my time to get work done. I didn't want to give up either one, so I decided that I needed to optimize myself. I had to adapt and get better. I had to achieve this perfect ideal that was out there somewhere, but mostly just floating around in my mind, the amalgamation of thousands of Instagram updates and Pinterest images. Surely there would be a trophy waiting for me at the end of this imaginary journey toward "perfect." Surely I would arrive, someday.

We make a lot of vows before we have kids, don't we? Some of the vows my husband and I made were:

Our kid is going to join our life, not vice versa. They are going to blend into our family rhythm. They are not going to become the center of our family.

We are never, ever getting a minivan. (So far, so good).

We will never let our kids disrupt a church service, movie, or any other assembly of adult humans. We will promptly remove them and administer needed discipline.

We are going to make sure our marriage is top priority.

We are going to spend time alone as a couple as much as possible.

Some of these vows we have managed to keep. But many of them were made before we had kids—and before kids changed us. When that child comes along, it is difficult to keep all the promises you made to yourself. You realize that "pre-parent" you was completely clueless. You are forced to compromise on some of your adult standards. You are forced to succumb to these tiny humans and their needs and wishes.

Life with kids is... messy. Before kids, I reveled in my tidy and pristine home. I would spend entire days deep-cleaning my house—and enjoying it. Tidy- that is how I like things. My house, my schedule, my friendships, my plans. Nice and tidy. If I could sweep it all up with a broom, polish it, shine it, and present it to the world, that is how I would do it.

But once kids come along, things just seem to explode. And it's not all bad. Kids explode the tidiness of our hearts. We can no longer fathom the limits of our love and devotion. We also struggle to understand the frustration, anger, and even resentment that they can arouse inside of us. But, whether good or bad, nothing is tidy anymore. And I am starting to wonder if the tidiness was all just an illusion all along—the illusion that I was in control.

It's kind of like baking.

I started baking with my daughter when she turned three. We would get out all the ingredients, mix the flour, butter, and eggs together, put our concoction in the oven, and a little while later something delicious would come out.

As you can imagine, baking with toddlers is a whole different ball game. The flour escapes the bag in a dust-like cloud and gets spread onto tiny fingers, which then lands all over the countertop in a fine white film. The eggs get cracked in a haphazard manner, causing tiny pieces of shell to go into the mix. Those same tiny flour-coated fingers want to try every possible ingredient before it goes into the bowl. There is no orderly way to go about it. It is managed chaos in every way.

But the end result is so very sweet.

Whenever I get the urge to bake, my daughter will inevitably crawl up on to the countertop, asking in her oh-so-sweet voice, "Mama, can I help?"

The pre-parent in me cringes. This could be so much easier and faster if I did it alone.

But the mama in me smiles and says yes—absolutely. I'll teach you how to bake, my girl, how to measure and dump and mix and keep things tidy. And you teach me how to taste the batter and turn the flour into a painting on the countertop and feel the squishy slime of the egg yolk between my fingers.

I'll teach you, and you teach me.

Maybe we need to keep saying yes, even when we cringe and would rather go the easier and tidier route. Maybe the mess is where the magic happens.

————

When my daughter was born, the nurses told me that she would need to eat every three hours. Through the night and early morning, they would bring her to me: twelve in the morning, three in the morning, six in the morning, until the sun slowly peeked through the window and a new day began. I was reminded of this when she was one year old and I decided to spend two days and nights at a Benedictine monastery. I watched as the monks gathered together to pray and chant every three hours of the day—through the day and night. And I remembered those nights, lying awake, feeding my daughter. There was a stillness and solitude that I can't explain. A bond was forged between us while the rest of the world slept. And now, at the monastery, I watched these monks woke in the middle of the night to hold the burdens of this world in their arms just like a mother holds her hungry baby. They awoke to pray and chant the Psalms, as they had been doing for centuries, and we awoke to feed and pray and sing our babies to sleep, just as mothers had been doing since time began. These monks were, in many ways, keeping watch, rocking and soothing the worries of the world just as a mother soothes her child. This parallel was not lost on me, and it struck me that just as God sees the monk waking and carrying the burdens of the world, he sees the mamas doing the tiring, monotonous, and holy work of mothering.

My entire life I have struggled with having quiet time with God. Yet as Christian mothers, we often feel pressure to be "in the Word" every single day. Before I had kids, it was just a matter of getting up early enough before work to actually spend more than five minutes in silence. I was one of those who would hit the snooze button until the very last opportunity, then spring out of bed and get ready as fast as I could. Now, as a mother of two, it is a matter of getting any time to myself. Getting up before my kids is typically a laughable scenario. I have never been much of a morning person, so when my alarm goes off, it's with the minimum amount of time required to get ready for the day. I spring into action immediately, my eyes still weary and my body groping for that morning cup of coffee. I shuffle the girls into clothes, make breakfast, and try to have some coherent conversation before we get moving. My time alone is sporadic at best, and my mornings are usually unpredictable and sleepy. Some mornings I can fit in a quiet time, but often it just doesn't happen.

Recently I stumbled upon the topic of "embodied prayer," the idea that we pray with our body—our hands, our feet, our actions—and not just our minds or our thoughts. The rationalism of modernist thought dominates our conceptions about prayer. When Paul said "pray without ceasing," he didn't literally mean that we should spend our entire day praying out loud to God, only speaking to God. I believe he meant that our lives should be the embodiment of prayer.

As mothers, we have the opportunity to do just this, to embody our prayers day in and day out. We use our hands to hold our children, to comfort them, to change their diapers, to change their clothes, to wipe tears and runny noses, to bathe them, to massage them, to stroke their heads, and to nourish them with bottle, breast, or food. Is this not prayer? Is this not a way of embodying our prayers to God and giving back to Him the honor and glory He deserves? When we serve our kids, we serve Him. There is honor and worship in that.

In Orthodox Judaism, there is even a blessing—the asher yatzar—recited when someone goes to the bathroom, thanking God for the human body, and another blessing— a netilat yadayim—recited upon washing hands![11] After a person leaves the bathroom, they wash their hands. According to Jewish etiquette, this should be done outside of the bathroom, but if there is no source of water available outside, it is permissible to wash one's hands inside the bathroom, then dry them outside.

The asher yatzar goes like this:

"Blessed are You, Hashem our God, King of the universe, who formed man with wisdom and created within him many openings and many hollows. It is obvious and known before Your Throne of Glory that if even one of them ruptures, or if even one of them becomes blocked, it would be impossible to survive and to stand before You (even for a short period). Blessed are You, Hashem, who heals all flesh and acts wondrously."

If this isn't a prayer for mothers, changing diapers day in and day out, I don't know what is.

———

A few years ago, my wonderful Uncle Melvin passed away. My husband and I decided to attend the funeral so that we could honor this amazing man's life and support my cousins in their grief and remembrance of him. Mel was Jewish, so this would be our first Jewish funeral. Afterward, we planned to attend a Shiva that my cousin was hosting at her home in the suburbs of Chicago. The night before we were to drive from South Bend to Chicago for the funeral, Evie started throwing up. We were staying with friends, so we quarantined ourselves upstairs so as not to infect them with this horrible virus. I was also pregnant at the time and hoping that I would not become the next victim.

That night, Matt became violently sick and threw up throughout the night and into the morning. Even though Matt was feeling extremely rough, we decided to hoof it to Chicago anyway. Matt climbed into the car, shaking, pale, and weak, and I loaded Evie into the backseat. We made it to the funeral, albeit a little late. Matt stayed in the car, and both he and Evie slept in the backseat.

After the funeral, we headed to my cousin's house for the shiva. I was excited to get to spend time with family I hadn't seen in a long time and eat some delicious nosh from the local deli. Matt decided to stay in the car during the event and continue to sleep off his wild night of digestive adventure. I loaded up my plate and Evie's plate with deli meats, crackers, cheese, and pickles. I was sure that Evie was feeling better and over her little virus. But I was wrong.

What happened next took place in slow motion. It was as though time stopped and all the energy and air in the room was sucked into a vacuum, a bubble, that could have been popped with a tiny needle. I turned around to give Evie another bite of food, but as she opened her mouth, she began to firehose vomit all over me. It wasn't just any throw-up situation, though. It was like a scene from the Exorcist. I was covered in vomit. Chairs began violently screeching away, and an awed, hushed silence came over the room as a few of my cousins swept in to help me figure out what to do first. Meanwhile, Evie continually wailed in my lap, "Mommy, I threw up! I threw up!"

By some small grace, I had packed a pair of jeans and my boots in the trunk of the rental car, so I went outside to get the clothes and let Matt know about the scene that had just unfolded in the house. He nodded at me in a feeble attempt at compassion. I honestly don't even think he heard me because he was so sick himself. I went back inside and sheepishly tried to clean up my daughter, the floor, and the table and chairs as the shocked and disgusted guests just stared in disbelief. I couldn't believe this was happening, especially during my uncle's shiva. We were supposed to be honoring his life; instead my family of three brought the projectile vomit show up from Nashville: And next, ladies and gentlemen, for your viewing enjoyment, Evie throwing up the turkey and cheese!

My cousin lent me a shirt from her closet, and we set out for home, all of us weak, battle weary, and not ready to drive back through Chicago at night. On the way home, I started feeling nauseous. You can imagine how this story ends—pregnant and throwing up all the next day and night.

Sometimes with kids you just can't pretend that you have it together. Sometimes all the decorum and self-respect you can muster is simply blown to bits at the most reverent and solemn of occasions because, well, you have kids. And you can only hope that you have some friends and family who will hold their noses and run toward the puke.

———

My husband and I were married young, twenty-one and twenty-three, to be exact. We both thought we knew everything, at least enough to get married. We knew what we needed to know, which was that we were desperately in love with each other, and we were best friends. We were a team. We were raised in the church, but we rejected the complementarian construct of marriage, which implies a hierarchical structure in the home with the husband at the top. We were both ready to take on marriage as a team of two equals with different skills. And for ten years, we did just that. We shared household duties: Matt cooked some nights; I did the laundry some weekends. We figured out what worked for us. But what no one told me was that as soon as I had kids, all of a sudden my role as "housewife," whether I worked or not, was going to expand exponentially.

There is a sociological term called the "double burden," which means women both handle the majority of caregiving and household management while also earning income for the household. I was feeling that double burden intensely, and before I knew it, I was a seething ball of resentment toward my husband. I don't think either of us even realized how to fix it at first. It wasn't as though he wasn't helpful, but it was just that he couldn't do as many things as I did because he was at work all day. He was in a dedicated space with adults, doing professional work. I had chosen to be home with my daughter, but the conflicting feeling arose when I then tried to work from home. Somehow my work wasn't real work because it was done in yoga pants and a ponytail.

It was as though the egalitarian life we had up to this point was subsumed by my motherhood role. Matt certainly couldn't breastfeed the baby, and he still had to go to work each morning, leaving me home with her.

It just made sense that this is what I would be doing. But then, resentment began to build. It felt like so much had changed for me in this transition, but not much had for him. Yes, he was getting less sleep because of the baby crying at night, and, yes, he was coming home to a much more exhausted wife who he had to pick up the slack for, but during the day, he still got to go out and have adult conversations. He got to sit at a computer and use his executive function. He got to have lunch meetings and go out after work for a drink if he wanted.

And although I was completely in love with my child, everything, especially when she was young, had to be planned around her feeding and nap schedule, her waking hours, even her happiness level on any given day. Most of the housework responsibilities landed on me, simply because I was home more. Our roles became more traditional out of necessity. However, I felt like I was becoming Donna Reed, and this was not what I had signed up for. I signed up to be a mom, but I didn't realize that along with that I now had to embrace the dated role of "homemaker." Being a homemaker wasn't something I necessarily bristled at. I loved decorating, making the house cozy, trying new recipes, and having people in our home. But when that role is placed upon you, even out of necessity, it takes away your power to choose. What happens then is that the things about homemaking that were once fulfilling and fun before kids, become routine and draining after kids.

It took Matt and I six years to find a new rhythm, and I will say that it gets easier as your children get older and their physical needs are less demanding. But early on, I decided that I wasn't going to just sit and seethe all the time. I was going to make my needs known. I was going to repeat, and remind, and ask until those needs were met. I wasn't going to pretend that I had it all together. One thing I realized early on is that my husband wanted to help, but he often worried that he wouldn't do a specific task to my standard so he didn't do it at all.

Instead of staying quiet and resenting my husband's existence, I began to ask for help. I began to explain. I began to stop telling myself that this was all up to me, that I was alone in this. It's hard to admit that we can't do it all at home, because if that is our primary and most important role in this life, what does that make us? Weak, failing, deficient. But this is a lie. Parenting is a team effort. We must step out from under the shame of asking for help from our own partners. We must humble ourselves enough to ask for help and to clearly communicate what we need. We must humble ourselves enough to be okay if they don't do it exactly how we would—if the onesie doesn't match the pants, if the hair bow is a little off kilter, if the highchair isn't wiped down perfectly. It's not fair to squash our partners attempts at support with our perfectionism.

Our own self-judgment can suffocate our efforts. Giving ourselves grace as we mother, do household tasks, and rewrite the narrative of how a parenting partnership can look is an important endeavor. With 75% of mothers in the workforce, it's way past time that the rules we conduct ourselves by at home begin to shift. I recognize that many of you reading this might be in a situation with your partner where they are less than willing to help, and this is not to put the burden squarely on your shoulders. It is just to say that if we never have the courage to express what we need, especially from those who love us most, we have a 100% chance of never getting it.

———

Adventure. That word may just be my favorite in the entire English language.

When I hear it, my whole body lights up with excitement. My mind is flooded with the most wonderful images—road trips, beautiful vistas, unknown bends in the trail, delicious food, and the sense that everything around me is new and pulsating with life. I may not know where I'll end up or what the journey will look like, but I am going somewhere. That sense of newness is what draws me to adventure, over and over again. It is what I crave. The experience of taking something in for the very first time, knowing that this isn't the place you inhabit day in and day out—that you are simply passing through, a wanderer who is there to take in the beauty and wisdom that this new place has to offer you.

This love of adventure and new experiences may have been part of the reason I waited ten years into my marriage to have children. To be honest, the thought of being "stuck" terrified me. I knew that traveling with kids was much more difficult, and many people told me that I might as well pack up my dream of an adventurous lifestyle once I became a mother. Despite the dire warnings I received, becoming a mother has done two things that I didn't quite expect: it has redefined my understanding of the word adventure and it has molded me into an even more adventurous person than I ever was before.

In those early days of motherhood when it was all I could do to grab a shower or a quick nap, I knew that instead of railing against my new reality, I needed to embrace the motherhood journey as the ultimate adventure in itself. If it was newness I sought, I surely gained that in the constantly changing features of my growing baby. If it was novelty, it was in the fleeting phases of development that seemed to arrive in constant waves, with me simply trying to keep up. My adventure had become quite small and even mundane in its activities, yes, but at the same time it seemed that the whole universe had become wrapped up in my daughter's tiny body. She was my adventure.

Now that I have two beautiful little girls and they have outgrown all their baby clothes, I find myself wanting to show them the world. Even more, I want to see the world through their eyes. Children operate in wonder. Their eyes haven't yet been dulled by the hardships of life, and that is a precious gift. Experiencing the world with them is like experiencing it completely anew.

So now, I take them outside as often as I can. We go down the street to the park to search for fairies, outside in the yard to check out the new spider web, or to the mountains to hike new paths and sit in awe beside thunderous waterfalls. They have made my life richer and more beautiful by being in it, and even the smallest outings can create the most beautiful memories.

For a time, certainly, I lost that sense of what I thought adventure was, and I mourned that loss. But now, I realize that there was so much more waiting on the other side, and I can't wait to see the whole world with my girls. There is so much beauty to show them.

CHAPTER 7

LEARNING TO LEAP

———

*All growth is a leap in the dark, a
spontaneous unpremeditated act
without benefit of experience.*

Henry Miller

It took most of my twenties for me to realize that I wasn't
cut out for working for someone else. I had never been
very good at it, but I always just thought I had a problem
respecting authority—or I was difficult. What I didn't
realize was that I had always had an entrepreneurial
spirit—wanting to sell things I had made as a child,
coming up with an idea for a local health food shop out
of college, or considering selling homemade bumper
stickers online in the early days of Etsy. I had always
loved business and the excitement of coming up with new
business ideas. It wasn't until I had a child that I had the
bravery to take the leap into entrepreneurship.

Eleven weeks after I had Evie, I got a job at the local National Public Radio affiliate. It was a temporary position, and my supervisor was so flexible and kind. I spent the majority of my day pumping in one of the editing bays. It was a bit of an awkward setup, and I brought along a hands-free pumping bra so that I could stuff envelopes or work on my laptop.

Let's talk for a minute about pumping. It is a big fat pain in the butt. No woman on this planet who pumps will tell you that it is something she enjoys doing. Hooking your boobs up to an electric machine that makes a strange whirring noise, audible to anyone within a one-hundred-foot radius, is just about one of the most awkward things ever. You feel like a Holstein, plain and simple.

There is the issue of sanitization. Everything must be washed in hot water before being used. And there are parts. Oh-so-many parts. You make sure they are washed the night before, so you don't have to wash them before you use them at work. You sit down in whatever location you have to pump—your own office, a nursing mothers' room, or a bathroom stall. Then, you put all the parts together—the tubing, the bottle, the suction cup. You hook your boobs up and put on the hands-free bra. And then you pump. You might get one ounce, you might get four. You just never know what the output is going to be. And then you tear down, wash up, and do it all over again three hours later.

Back to the radio station editing bay. I was all set up, machine whirring, milking away. Just folding envelopes, being super productive. Making one of the most nutrient-dense foods on earth to feed my baby—and earning money at the same time!

I was clearly winning.

But then something happened- a phone rang in the editing bay.

And I heard a very persistent knock on the door. "I need to get that call!" I heard a news reporter yell into the bay.

Holy crap! No!

"Do you not see the sign?!"

(The handmade sign I had constructed was the equivalent of a grown-up "Keep Out!" sign. It also served to cover a small window on the door so that no one got an unintended peep show.)

More banging. More ringing.

"I need to get that call!"

"Do not open that door unless you want to see something you can never unsee!" I screamed frantically as I whipped off the pump, breastmilk flying, put my bra back on, fastened my shirt buttons, and answered the phone calmly and collectedly with a "hello, how can I help you?"

On the other end: "Yes, I am calling for the interview with..."

Me, voice trembling with horror: "Yes, absolutely. Let me get him for you. One moment please."

I opened the door, completely mortified and my team member felt the same. We exchanged the most awkward half-second glance of all time as we slid past each other in the doorway.

This, my friends, is the reality of pumping in the workplace.

That may have been the moment I decided it was time to officially start my own business.

———

When I first got started, I had no clue what I was doing. Not one clue. I knew I needed a plan. I mean, after all, I had attended a four-year university and earned a degree in music business, with the emphasis on business. I knew that no successful business started out without a plan. Plus, I loved planning! So, when Evie was about one year old, I decided to take a weekend trip away to create my business plan.

At that point, I had begun work on my graduate degree in theology before she was born, continued taking classes while pregnant, brought her to my on-campus classes when I needed to, and had a great deal of help from my mom and in-laws. I knew I wanted to earn an advanced degree because, let's face it, I loved school and never wanted college to end. So I decided I would learn about the thing that was most important to me— the mysteries of God and Scripture. The practicalities of this were minimal at best, considering I had no intent on becoming a pastor, but at the time it just made sense. Some of my classmates were already pastors or had been in ministry for years, so this pursuit was much more practical for them. But, for me, it was just an experiment in curiosity—a very expensive one, I might add. As in, around $50,000 expensive. But we can get to the debt mountain story later.

I would go to classes one week per semester in Virginia Beach and complete the remainder of my courses online, at home. There were lots of big books with intimidating titles like *Advanced Hermeneutics and Homiletics*. My friends got used to hearing me say, "Sorry I can't come. I have to study." It took me six years to finish that degree, and I honestly didn't know what I was going to do with it except that the subject matter interested me immensely. I was able to study under some amazing professors, have experiences with classmates that would shape me forever, and bring my daughter along for the ride, even though she was too young to remember.

Something about going to school near the beach was magical as well. We got to take strolls along the empty boardwalk in October, and then I got to go and immerse myself in a beautiful library full of books—the collective writing of so many people with profound thoughts. Libraries have always had my heart. I took them for granted during my time as an undergraduate, but now that I had been in the workforce a few years and seen how "real life" works—the daily grind, doing the same thing day after day just to make rent—I would nearly cry when I entered a library. It felt like I was entering a different world, a magical place where ideas were the currency and curiosity the only payment for entry. They were pure magic to my soul.

I came across the idea of a silent retreat in one of my graduate school classes. It seemed like a very spiritual thing to do, and something that was naturally discussed among students who were all pursuing this ethereal and not-so-practical degree with me. I was dying to try one. Granted, I am the last possible candidate for a silent retreat. My mouth is constantly moving. I could talk to a rock as long as my thoughts were somehow finding their way out of my mind and into open air. And if my mouth wasn't moving, my mind was—never stopping, always making connections and coming up with new ideas. It's exhausting really. The thought of a weekend of silence was daunting, but also intriguing.

I decided it was time to go for it, and there was no other way I was going to be able to crank out my business plan without some dedicated time alone. So I booked a room at a Benedictine Monastery for a weekend in May. I left Evie, who was only one year old, with Matt, and I ventured to Kentucky for my silent retreat. Although I knew it would be a challenge, I was looking forward to it, as I had been feeling somewhat dry in my spiritual life.

On my way there, I listened to as much music as I could, blasting my favorite tunes. The thought of going without any auditory stimulation for an entire whole weekend was downright terrifying to me. When I arrived that Friday evening, I headed straight into the 7:30 Compline Service. The monks filed in, took their places, and began to chant the Psalm. My initial reaction was unexpected; I recoiled at the repetition and simplicity of it all. The monks' lifestyle was such a stark contrast to mine. Everything I valued seemed to be challenged by their very existence: speed, achievement, personal ambition, newness, adventure, collecting memories and experiences. I couldn't believe these men could be truly happy, and I was put off by that thought, even though I couldn't deny thinking it. They pray seven times a day, live in silence, work, eat, read, and sleep. That is all. Every. Single. Day.

The silence is unnerving at first. The first night, I kept waking up, thinking about Matt or Evie or a client, and my chest would tighten. *What do they need? What should I be doing right now?* Then I would realize there were no obligations.

It took a few hours for the noise in my mind to finally clear away so that I could truly begin to hear my own thoughts, uncluttered. I could also hear the sounds of nature—the birds, the stream, the flies buzzing, the woodpecker, the otter scampering along, the owl. The sounds of worship. Other than that, the only other sounds I heard were that of the monks chanting the Psalms and this refrain. "Praise the Father, the Son, and Holy Spirit, both now and forever... the God who is, who was, and is to come, at the end of the ages." The sounds of worship.

The whole place was like a breath of fresh air to my soul. My heart had room to expand. By the afternoon of day two, I found myself cherishing the silence. My heart slowed down. My thoughts slowed down. My mind was quiet and at peace. I found myself driven to repentance on many occasions. I was so overwhelmed by the sheer magnitude of God's presence and mercy there. I took refuge under His wings and hid myself in Him. And His Spirit ministered to my Spirit in ways unspeakable and un"write"able. In the silence, God came near.

An old Gaelic Rune of Hospitality goes,

> *I saw a stranger yestereen:*
> *I put food in the eating place,*
> *Drink in the drinking place,*
> *Music in the listening place:*
> *And in the sacred name of the Triune*
> *He blessed myself and my house,*
> *My cattle and my dear ones.*
> *And the lark said in her song,*
> *Often, often, often*
> *Goes the Christ in the stranger's guise.*
> *Often, often, often*
> *Goes the Christ in the stranger's guise.*

Following the Rule of St. Benedict, the monks receive everyone as Christ himself. I was given a place to sleep and three square meals a day at no cost to myself, except the travel to get there. Having worked in a place where the value of hospitality was practiced every day, it was interesting to be the "stranger" who was the recipient of this radical hospitality. I spent my mornings in my room, my meals eaten in silence, and my afternoons under a huge oak tree writing in my journal. In the evenings I would go to my room, sit at my computer, and type out my business plan.

The silence was golden.

When I returned home and was talking to my husband

about the experience, he asked me an important question: "But what do these monks do for the outside world?" After a moment, I came to this conclusion: "they exist. They are a witness to the truth and presence of God in a culture and world that ignores the spiritual in so many ways."

———

During this time, I was part of a program called Dream Year, where my friend named Ben hosted a group of us in his home in Virginia Beach. The fact that I went to school there was somewhat serendipitous, as I was able to meet with Ben and he technically became my first client. He ran a creative conference called STORY, and I reached out to him via email after hearing about the Dream Year program. He agreed to offer me a paid freelance role, managing the conference's social media, and I happily accepted. That was the first time I'd ever received money for my work on a freelance basis. I thought he would walk away, or laugh in my face when I made the offer, but he said yes. And that was one of the most important "yeses" I've ever received.

Working for STORY, I had the opportunity to attend a weekend conference for the Dream Year program. Ben hosted a group of people in his home to learn together, listen to speakers, and enjoy some delicious meals and experiences. He was a producer at heart, and had a knack for creating environments and spaces where people could truly connect and be inspired. I sat in that room with other creative entrepreneurs drinking up every single ounce of wisdom I could take in. It was magical.

After that event, I had several talks with Ben about how well the STORY social media was going and how this could become work that I could monetize as a sustainable business. He helped me design the best way to arrange my service packages, and made the first few calls so I could obtain new clients. Once I got my first "yes," I knew it was time to leap. I quit my job at NPR. For the time, I had enough income to replace my part-time work. I knew it wasn't guaranteed, but is any income truly "guaranteed"? I started. That is often the hardest part.

Leaping is different than jumping or hopping. Leaping is doing it with boldness, holding both fear and courage in your heart, knowing there may or may not be a net beneath you. It's not like jumping gingerly over a puddle. I didn't know what would happen, but I knew I couldn't keep doing what I was doing. I knew that if I stayed where I was, I would wither. I knew my daughter was counting on me to not play it small. And if I failed, then I'd just "pick myself up, dust myself off, and start all over again," as Fred Astaire sang.[12] I had to do it. The time was right.

It was exhilarating and terrifying- everything a leap should be.

I remember jumping out of a plane on my eighth wedding anniversary with my husband. The plane ride up was the most torturous part. The waiting, the knowing you were going to jump soon, and then what? Sitting in the door hatch and looking down, convincing yourself that you've come this far, don't look back now. Just jump..

Once you are falling, sheer terror and then exhilaration take over. The adrenaline wins out. You feel more alive than ever, and you wonder why you hadn't done this before.

Sometimes you just have to take a leap. Invest the cash. Get the loan. Take the course. Send the email. Ask for the thing you want. We can easily masquerade as responsible adults when we are actually just afraid of taking a risk. What does your leap look like?

CHAPTER 8

BUILDING MY OWN FORT

What you don't know can
be your greatest asset.

Sara Blakely

In the career books of this decade and the last, the entire genre is replete with advice for women on how to act like men. As much as those books tried to be helpful, the advice they offer is unhelpful at best and appalling at worst. It offers only black and white stereotypes of women's behavior in the workplace. Women are taught to wear pantsuits, give a firm handshake, and not get too emotional in meetings. They are taught that being a woman in the workplace is an automatic detriment to them, so they must hide it.

I don't believe that women need to learn how to

survive in a male-dominated corporate environment. We can make our own working worlds that reflect who we are on a deeply holistic level. We don't need to learn how to be more manly or more assertive to succeed. We need to be 100% ourselves—in life and in business. Unapologetic and unashamed. We are mothers, we are nurturers, and we are badass.

When I initially went back to work after having Evie, it was absolute torture leaving her that first morning. It felt wrong in a million different ways, as though I was leaving an appendage at home and wishing it the best of luck surviving on its own. I hated pumping, so I always only had just enough to get her through the day, and often I would have to wake up multiple times in the night to pump enough for the next day.

One particular day, it took me over two hours to get home due to crazy Nashville traffic. I called my mom and she was frantic. "She's starving, honey. You have to get home!" I could hear Evie crying in the background, and I panicked. I was sobbing and pounding the steering wheel. My baby was hungry, and I couldn't get to her. It was the worst possible feeling I have ever experienced as a mother—so helpless, so desperate. When I got home, I held her to my breast, nursed her, and calmed her tears. She finally got what she had been so frantically needing, and I got what I needed too. I was with her. I was nourishing her. Nobody else could give her what I could. And that is a powerful biological and evolutionary urge. No matter how much equality women gain in culture and the workplace, that powerful primal urge cannot, and should not be removed. It is what has kept humanity going for centuries.

Years ago, when I read that Marissa Mayer, the former CEO of Yahoo, was going back to work after two weeks of maternity leave, I didn't see her as an empowered woman who was making her own choices. I saw her as a woman who was caught up in a toxic corporate culture. Because as any mother would tell you, no woman wants to go back to work at two weeks postpartum. At two weeks postpartum, you want a lot of things—a decent night's sleep, hormone balance, jeans that fit, adult conversation, and more coffee. What you do not want is any level of responsibility beyond keeping the tiny creature alive that just came out of your body.

I am speaking from experience. At three weeks postpartum with my second child, I went back to work. Now to be fair, I was working from home, barely part time. But that alone was enough to send me over the edge. I did want some adult interaction, and getting to exercise the higher functioning parts of my brain did feel good. When you have a small child, you are in primal mode. Survival is the name of the game. So getting to do some writing and client interaction was nice. But to go back to work full time at two weeks postpartum? I don't see how that is helpful to anyone—the mother, the baby, or the organization you are serving.

I agree with the fact that women in the upper echelons of corporate America can make a difference in the companies they work for if they make it high enough up the ladder or into the boardroom. But is this the path that all women must take to make a difference? I don't believe so.

As a woman, I run my business as myself. I don't change who I am for my clients, male or female. My clients appreciate my warmth and candor. They do not seem to be uncomfortable with the way that I do business. They know that they can shoot straight with me, and I can shoot straight with them. I have a no-nonsense approach to business, and my clients don't seem put off by me making a bit more casual conversation, or letting them know I have to quiet down my child in the next room. As women, we typically don't silo or compartmentalize our lives. We see the parts of our lives as holistic, linked, connected, and interchangeable.

In *Lean In*, Sandberg described the current business culture, not as a ladder but as a jungle gym. She basically throws women a few bones and wishes them the best of luck as they meander around on this jungle gym, trying to make it to the top without getting thrown off. But you know what I say? Screw the jungle gym. You will not find me scrambling along any jungle gym, thank you very much.

I know it's not a question of either/or; it's both/and. The way companies view mothers has to change, and the way we view work as a whole needs to change. But when Sandberg says that careers are a jungle gym, not a ladder, I can't help but think to myself, *I don't want to climb either one.* I'm just going to be over here building my own fort. It's going to be the kind of place you don't have to climb to get into. You can just come on in, sit down, and play.

We can construct this fort together, all of us. We don't have to hustle to meet the world's definition of success.

This fort is my own company, where we create cohesive brand stories for businesses. In this fort, I can hire women who are highly skilled, highly intelligent, and have a ton of heart. I can pay them well—what they are worth and then some. They can work on their own time. And be with their kids. They don't have to play by the rules over at the jungle gym.

In our fort, we play by a whole different set of rules. We don't have to leave our womanhood at the door to succeed. We don't have to learn to have a firmer handshake or a more resolute gaze. We don't have to pretend our mothering is a secondary priority. We can be ourselves, in all of our humanity.

Is there still hard work? Of course. Is there frustration and tension? Yes. Is there struggle? Absolutely. It's the kind that gives you a good, long, fulfilling sigh at the end of the day. Another day's work—babies comforted and nursed, happy clients served, meals made, diapers changed, video calls carried out with only a few glitches, important words written down, books read, deals made, and all of it running together into one beautiful, messy, redemptive portrait.

I made the choice to walk the line and start my own business. And let me tell you, the walk is a tightrope between two high rises. The stakes are high, and you sweat a lot. You wonder if you are doing the right thing, if maybe you should turn back. But once you are there, the thrill of it takes over. And you know you have to keep going.

I choose to be present with my kids when I am with them. And I choose to spend intentional time away from them to pursue my dreams.

I believe mothers are not hindered in their dual callings and vocations, but they are given a special grace that allows them to be even more productive, more goal-oriented, and more focused than anyone else. I believe when it comes to pursuing our dual callings, we are not at a disadvantage, but we actually have several advantages:

1. Creativity: Simply being in the presence of children causes us to open our eyes to the wonder of creation. We see things differently. We stop, we sit, we listen, we marvel. This is the wellspring of all creativity. If you ever feel dried up creatively, you need only to spend an hour with a toddler, pretending and exploring.

2. Play: Our children teach us how to play again, and all innovation comes from the freedom we experience in play. Play is the furthest thing from wasting time—it is a valuable commodity. Without play, we cannot come up with new ideas. We cannot remember what really matters. We cannot innovate. As moms, we have at our daily disposal what major corporations such as Google and Lego spend millions to cultivate—a sense of play and wonder.

3. Urgency: Mothers know that when the children are napping or playing quietly, we have a set amount of time to accomplish something. We do not have the luxury of putting off priority items until later. As moms, we don't get a later. Later will bring with it a myriad of new responsibilities. We get right now.

4. Focus: This goes hand-in-hand with the above. When mothers do get any amount of free time, we can typically laser-focus on what needs to get done. We know how to knock things off the list, and quickly.

5. Planning Ahead: Moms throughout the land know the panic that can ensue when caught out at a restaurant without a diaper or baby wipes, or the horror of forgetting a pacifier at home when your child is screaming in the backseat. We know the importance of planning ahead. We don't forget to plan ahead, because the stakes are too high.

There have been many articles written about this phenomenon recently, but it's something mothers have known forever. Because of the limits placed on our time, we are more productive. Mothers should never be underestimated. Even in the 1950s and '60s, when Avon, the skincare and beauty product company became a household name, women were finding ways to utilize their gifts, talents, and passions to either provide supplemental income for their families or simply do something they enjoyed that gave them a sense of community.

What if the scripts we have been taught about business are simply that, scripts? Scripts that need to be rewritten. The workforce is already changing rapidly to accommodate remote employees, and the trend in the job market is toward self-employment and a gig economy. Corporations who are updating their policies to better support parents and caregivers are sadly still the exception, not the rule.

Fathers want to parent, too, and have the flexibility to be available for their children's lives while they are still young. Mothers are engaged in the workforce at record rates (75% as of 2018) and need partners who are able to parent with them on an equal playing field. As the corporate world continues to change to adapt to these new realities, some of us have decided we'd rather jump ship. We are better off on our own, we say. And yes, there are trade-offs. I haven't had decent health insurance in years. The security of a paycheck being deposited into my bank account each month isn't necessarily there, but I have the freedom to attend my kid's class parties and field trips while also accomplishing work during the day, without having to explain to a boss where I was. I am not a slave to anyone else's clock but my own.

I will never forget when I started my company. A close friend of mine, who had already made her foray into the freelance world, told me that now I would be wearing two hats. Employee Hilary and CEO Hilary. And I had to manage myself like a CEO. I had to think like both.

I read all the business and productivity books I could get my hands on—*The E-Myth Revisited*[13] being the most impactful one—and soaked up as much knowledge as I could. The mindset shift from hourly or salary employee to CEO is huge.

I realized that when I worked for others, I wasn't being paid for my productivity. I was being paid just to be in that physical space and somehow signal to my coworkers and boss that I was "working." Now that I was responsible for my own revenue generation, things changed drastically. There was no time at all for screwing around. My time was precious, my business's success was at stake, and I had to get things done. I began to track my time and my work habits and realized that I had some pretty awful ways of procrastinating. Starting a business, and the highs and lows of running one became the crucible inside which my entire professional outlook was formed.

The first thing I began to do was to track what I was working on and for how long. This helped me see if I was spending my time on the most important things. In applying the Pareto Principle to my work, I knew that 80 percent of my revenue should come from 20 percent of my focused efforts.[14] So it was important to make sure I was spending my time doing things that mattered. I had to ask myself hard questions about what types of clients I wanted to take on, and the types of people I wanted around me to support my growing business.

Of course, in the first few years, it was a constant balancing act between time and money. I would have loved to have been able to hire an administrative assistant to handle all my scheduling and logistics, but that wasn't financially possible. I handled everything from sales to accounting to client relationships, and it was insane, but I loved every minute of it. I learned so much in that first year about simply trusting my instincts and making sure I was on top of my schedule so I could get the necessary work done. And you know what? It felt so good to be my own boss, to be providing for my family without having to miss the huge moments in my daughters' lives that I knew were so important.

I am so grateful that I had the opportunity to create a sustainable business that worked for me during the most tender phase of my girls' lives. The phrase "do what you love and you'll never work a day in your life" is a lie, because you will work harder than you ever have. But it won't always feel like work; it will feel like something that fills you up rather than deflates you. It will be something that doesn't have you dreading Monday morning, but looking forward to it. That is a gift, and it's something that any mother should have the opportunity to do if she so chooses.

As mothers, we spend most of our time hunched over, our shoulders concave. We bend over to do most everything—to nourish our children with our breasts, to change diapers and outfits, to hand out snacks, to stir over a stove, to protect, hold, and snuggle our young ones. This is a place that we must live for some time. But sooner or later, that bending is going to take a toll on our bodies. We were born to walk upright. We were created to face the sun, head on.

There is beauty in the bending, and there is care. But when I began to stand up, open my shoulders wide, and smile back at the sun, I began to feel life come back into me again. I could greet the world with open arms and an open heart. I could bend over and protect, nourish, feed, and soothe when I needed to, but then I could stand back up again. I could straighten up, look my own life in the face with honesty, and not live in that protected and curled up place all the time. We must be able to do both. We are not meant to completely fold under the weight of it all. We must reach out our hands to others, and our hearts to what's ahead. There is hope there. There is freedom when we open ourselves up to what is possible.

CHAPTER 9

THE BLESSING IN THE BREAKING

―――――

Ring the bells that still can ring
Forget your perfect offering
There is a crack in everything
That's how the light gets in.

Leonard Cohen, "Anthem"

My second daughter's birth went almost as badly off the rails as her sister's. I had hoped and planned for a natural VBAC (Vaginal Birth after Ceasarean), but once I arrived at my forty-second week of pregnancy, my midwives told me that my chances of having a successful labor were very slim. So on Wednesday, September 10, 2014 I woke up early, took a shower, put on my makeup, and drove to the hospital for a scheduled Repeat Caesarean.

A strange silence filled the car on our way there. Once we were checked in, the nurses began to get me into a gown and take my vitals. Resident after resident came in to introduce themselves, along with the surgeons, anesthesiologists, and the amazing nurse who would be helping us with the "family-friendly" procedure. Finally, they wheeled me into the operating room and administered the spinal anesthesia. The procedure went much longer than Evie's, and I began to get agitated. I just wanted to meet my daughter. Not to mention that the head surgeon murmured the words "oh shit" while I was open on the table. Not something you want to hear during surgery. My spinal had been administered while my legs were hanging in a funny position on the table, so my agitation only increased as I tried to "lift" my legs back onto the table, although they were already there and my brain just hadn't processed it. I was yelling at the top of my lungs "TESSA! WHERE IS MY TESSA GIRL!" and finally, after what seemed like an eternity, she appeared to me. She screamed the most high-pitch velociraptor-sounding scream, that the entire Labor and Delivery floor heard it. I held my baby girl in my arms after ten months of waiting and preparing for her! Despite the intensity of this birth experience, it was such an amazing feeling. Once we returned home, we settled into our new normal with our two beautiful daughters. I thought life would be wonderful. And it was—at least mostly—for about six months. And then it wasn't.

———

Nashville summers are brutal. The Southern heat is

relentless, heavy, sticky like honey. It hits you like a wave the minute you step outside. It pulls you down into itself, making you feel like every step you are taking is into a pool of molasses. You move more slowly, your muscles feel heavy, and everything hangs in the air with the weight of the humidity. After ten years in the South I've learned to embrace it. There are ways to cope—lighter clothing, hair ties, high-powered deodorant, comfortable sandals. But nothing can prepare you for the kind of heat that happens during a Tennessee summer. This summer was my end... and my beginning. This was the summer when everything fell apart.

I was six months postpartum with Tessa, when I began to have a massive migraine as well as panic attacks. My vision went haywire. I assumed it was hormonal and a result of stress, exhaustion, or typical postpartum depression. But even then, something felt different about this. I couldn't explain it, but it was as if something had invaded my brain. I didn't feel like myself. had been pacing along, pretending that Tessa's birth was simply a minor adjustment to my schedule. I was making client calls at three weeks postpartum, writing content, staying up until 3:00 a.m. working on projects, getting up to nurse Tess in the middle of the night, then sleeping for a few hours and waking up to do it all over again. I was trying to hold it all together. I was living on coffee. My adrenals were apparently over it and didn't give me any warning before they went on permanent strike.

The week all this began, I received two large spider bites on both of my ankles. They concerned me somewhat, but I never in my wildest dreams imagined that there could be any connection between the bites and my psychological symptoms. I applied some essential oils to them to help speed the healing process, and it took them over one month to heal. The skin tissue around the bites turned gray. I didn't know what bit me, but I knew it wasn't your typical garden-variety spider.

A few weeks later, I spiked a 103-degree fever. I chalked it up to the flu and moved on. And that's when the visual symptoms began. First, visual snow. Then diminished night vision, afterimages, haloes, and then, eventually, everything around me just looked double and blurry. It was as if I were seeing the world around me through a smoky screen, all the time. But my panic and anxiety were so debilitating that I could barely get in the car with my children and drive down the street to the park. I didn't eat for days. I could feel myself spiraling into a long-term panic attack. My head pounded as if someone had taken a hatchet right down the middle, and I was in bed, writhing in pain.

I could feel myself sinking deeper and deeper, and I didn't know what to do to stop it. All the work, the sleepless nights, the adrenaline, the constant fight or flight, and the recovery from childbirth and major surgery had caught up to me. My body was done, and these spider bites, as I would come to find out, tipped the scales. I laid in bed and just thought, *This is it. I'm done. I'm down for the count, and not coming back up.* I went over to a close friend's house with my kids, and she force-fed me granola bars and water while our children played, unaware of the craziness that was going on inside my head and my body. I was terrified that something neurological was going on and insisted on seeing a neurologist to rule out something serious. But going to the doctor only reinforced my fear.

There was something wrong with me, and I couldn't fix it.

As I looked back over the prior three years, I realized that my anxiety had been continually mounting ever since my first daughter was born. Then, having my second daughter simply pushed me over the edge. No amount of avoiding, working, or pretending it away was going to overcome the deep postnatal depletion, both mentally and physically, that I was experiencing. This was going to be a long journey out of the dark, and I wasn't remotely prepared for it.

I went to two neurologists and two ophthalmologists. They told me I was having migraines, but I knew that was not what was happening. Being at the premier hospital in the South and having experts in their field look at you with a sense of confusion in their eyes is something I will never forget, a sense of being so very lost. I knew at that moment I was on my own. At my neurologist appointment later that week, I asked the doctor about Zoloft. I was so desperate for relief, I didn't know what else to do. I felt like a failure—like I wasn't able to be my best for my kids. But I knew I needed something to simply take the edge off of life. I heard someone say that with panic and anxiety, everything just feels sharp, jagged, and scary. Nothing is safe; nothing is okay. Even the little things. And I needed something to smooth out the edges.

So I took the plunge. That following Sunday, I went to church, and as we sang, "God, you're all I need," I thought, *Well, yes. God and Zoloft.* God, plus a medication to keep me from being a panic-stricken, depressive mess. Having grown up in the church, I understood the stigma about taking psychological medications from an early age. Taking medication for mental health was something you did not discuss. It was a private matter. Having to take meds meant that your faith wasn't strong enough, your beliefs weren't big enough, your trust in God wasn't solid enough. It meant you had failed somehow. At least that was what I told myself. But I knew that without this medication, I wouldn't get through the day. I wouldn't be able to perform even the most basic activities to keep my family going. I had to have it.

So I swallowed the Zoloft and waited for it to take effect.

And just like that, I became numb, and that in itself was a form of temporary relief, although the feelings of dread and negativity didn't stop. Each time I would sit down to nurse my baby in her darkened room, the monsters in my mind would start talking. They would say horrible things—untrue things. Dreadful, frightening, highly unlikely scenarios would play out in my mind. Fear consumed me. I thought I would never again see the light of day, even though it was summer and the sun wouldn't stop shining. My world was dark as night.

Everything inside felt like it was dying, like this was going to be the end of me. I couldn't look forward to anything. As hard as I tried, nothing brought me joy. I would watch my girls playing, and even laugh with them, but it was hollow. I had always been the person who would wake up in the morning with such a strong sense of hopefulness, of purpose, of expectation, of joy. But I couldn't access those emotions. They were simply gone. The Zoloft helped me function—to let go of what didn't truly matter. It smoothed the edges, but I knew it wasn't going to fix what was broken deep down inside of me, in my cells, in my bones.

Eventually, I would begin to experience other neurological symptoms—tremors, memory loss, inability to find my words, typing errors, and clumsiness. I started knocking things over in the kitchen and feeling like I didn't have control over my body. I started feeling pins and needles in my hands and feet. For one whole year, I just dealt with it. I felt like I was retreating further and further inside myself. I didn't know what to do or what was wrong with me. I went to every specialist—medical and alternative—to try and treat my "visual snow." I researched and researched, joined Facebook groups, and got my hands on any information I could. I went to therapy to overcome my anxiety and experienced some intense emotional healing there.

And then one weekend, it hit me.

We were taking a hike in the woods with the girls, and, at this point, I had begun to have increasing feelings of depersonalization and derealization. It was as if I were watching my life play out in front of me like a movie. We were at our favorite place to hike, Radnor Lake, and I remember looking at the girls, and feeling so happy, but also feeling like I wasn't actually experiencing my own life. Like my emotions had to be conjured up. Like I was separate from myself. If you have never experienced it, it's hard to understand. But it is a terrifying feeling.

Then it hit me! The puzzle pieces started coming together. All of my symptoms began right after I received the spider bites on my ankles. Surely that couldn't cause something like this, right? No way. I had already e-mailed my doctor about the possibility of Lyme Disease, and I shrugged it off because I was sure that they weren't tick bites.

So I made an appointment with my doctor, who just happened to be the only Lyme-Literate MD in the state of Tennessee. I feared my hunch being confirmed, but also my doctor saying, "I'm not sure what you have. You'll need to go see a neurologist and get a scan." He ran bloodwork and my labs came back somewhat inconclusive. Although they did show evidence of previous exposure, my doctor was not comfortable using the term "diagnosis." However, he did say that he felt comfortable treating me for Bartonella, which is a coinfection of Lyme disease that can be spread by a particular spider. But it all felt so mushy, so unclear. Like maybe he wasn't even sure.

In that moment, I felt vindicated and robbed all at once. Everything changed, and nothing changed. "Bartonella" sounded so... weird. It wasn't even the name of a disease. It was the name of a bacteria. So my illness was the name of the bacteria, transferred by some nasty spider into my immune-suppressed body? I couldn't get a fancier diagnosis—something more recognizable? Where were the ribbons, the community support, the fundraisers, the 5k walks? Nothing. All I got was a resounding silence.

When it comes to everything, and especially my health, I need firm edges on things. I want things to have a name, a plan, a clear-cut narrative. The messy middle is not my jam. I also was in a state of shock, not because it wasn't what I expected, but because it was now a real thing. I went over and over in my emotions—acceptance, rejection, shock, depression, obsession. I vacillated between allowing it to consume my thoughts completely and ignoring it altogether.

At the same time, I found out that I have a specific genetic mutation called methylenetetrahydrofolate reductase, or MTHFR (which, you can guess what I call it among friends). It explains so much about how my whole life, I have been more sensitive than others to environmental toxins. Why I feel like I can never get away with anything, whether it's greasy food, drinking, or anything that might throw my system out of whack. It explains why this bacteria was able to get a foothold in my body in the first place. At first, I freaked out. I didn't want this to define me. I didn't want it to change me. I wanted no part of it.

Then I realized something: We so often don't get to choose our own stories. They choose us. We only get to choose how we respond. So instead of hating it, wondering "why me?," and kicking against it, I decided I would learn what the experience had to teach me. I may never know why, but I do know that nothing is lost on God. It isn't naive to hold on to hope. It's a human necessity. It's as important as breathing in and out.

This was something I had feared for so long. My close friends, if they are being honest, would say I definitely had heath anxiety. I have always been terrified by disease, illness, something that threatens to not only kill you, but to take away your quality of life. And now that I have lived through a disease that did just that, fear can still creep in. I am learning every day to overcome it. This disease tried to steal my very mind—my ability to express myself, to play with my kids, to speak clearly and think clearly, to have the energy and stamina to live and thrive.

The thought of having to recognize it and treat it scared me. It meant that it was real. But it was also something I couldn't allow to consume me and define me. The disease was something that happened to me, something that shaped my identity, my perspective, and my life, forever. Instead of fearing it, I chose (over and over again) to learn what it had to teach me. I am a body, made of microbes and matter, and these particular little nasty microbes were doing their best to survive inside of me. I had no intention of letting them, and the fight was very bitter, even ugly. But I didn't quit.

During that time, I wrote the following entry in my journal:

MAY 3, 2015

This past week has been... whoa. I have felt as though this was coming, but when it came, it seemed to have completely blindsided me. In many ways I am still in the midst of it. As much as I want this to be over, I know it's not something that will be quick. I knew that the minute it began. The things I relied on were no longer available to hold me up. Whatever glue that was keeping all my pieces intact gave way. And I fell apart. But maybe it's when we fall apart that we are able to see that what was holding us together wasn't all that sturdy and reliable to begin with. Maybe we realize that what we thought was crazy glue was just one of those cheap glue sticks that kids use to paste tissue onto construction paper.

All my life I have been afraid of that dark feeling that can come over me sometimes. The feeling that all is lost. Hopelessness. Despair. It feels like the complete absence of God—maybe what Hell would feel like. And I never want to have that feeling again.

But maybe what I fear as death or dying is really just separation. Isolation. That is the most difficult thing about suffering isn't it? It's that sometimes we simply have to do it alone. We can have deep connection with others, even in the midst of it, but that pain is our own. And in that dark place of suffering, the only one who can penetrate the isolation is God's Spirit.

The only possible way to not feel alone is to know that the God who understands suffering is not only with us, but in us as we go through it. The triune God who only knows communion is communing inside of us. And darkness is not dark to Him. We are never alone. Even in the valley of the shadow of death, His Spirit ushers us, guides us, leads us with a gentle hand into glory.

Psalm 139:11–12 says, "If I say, 'surely the darkness will hide me, and the light around me will become night'—even the darkness is not dark to you. The night shines like the day; darkness and light are alike to you" (CSB).

The darkness is not dark to Him, even the deepest darkness, the kind that covers us over like a cold blanket and keeps us from seeing anything in front of us, even our own hand. Even when the darkness isolates us completely, the night shines like the day. There is no darkness that God's light cannot penetrate and turn into a day that is shining with glorious rays of sun.

I had lived my entire life up to that point in a dualism of mind and body. My mind was me, and my body was just the vehicle for getting me (my thoughts, my will) enacted in the world. But my body finally encountered a crisis that I couldn't ignore. I realized that my body wasn't just a vehicle, a shell, or something to be mastered or perfected. My body was me. And it was done with my nonsense.

I promptly dove into as many healing modalities as I could fit into my schedule. I attended yoga classes, went to acupuncture appointments, and faithfully took my medication. I began researching mindfulness and meditation to help calm my mind and my body. I read about the mind/body connection and the impact of trauma on the brain and the body. And I began to connect some dots around how I came to find myself in such a state of brokenness.

Fear pushes you into a corner and tries to isolate you from your story. Your story has power, even in the suffering. Even in the losses. The message that fear and depression try to trick you into believing is not that you will always suffer, but that your suffering doesn't have meaning. That is the biggest lie of all.

———

Every time I open social media, I am introduced to the story of someone's suffering. Someone's child is terminally ill. Someone shares a hashtag that honors someone's child who ran out into the street and was tragically killed by an automobile. Someone shares a gory video of how checking your phone on the highway can kill you instantly. Mothering forums share every nature of their children's medical issues, with advice on what they did and the specific outcomes. (Side note: I can't think of a single time, in all my scrolling of forums, when I actually received any measure of comfort or helpful advice.)

All of these things are happening. And all of them are absolutely tragic and terrible. But the question is: has social media and the widespread use of the internet created a commodity out of tragedy and trauma? The thing about trauma is that it's very nature is sudden and unexpected. It's not just the event that is the trauma, but the unexpectedness of it. You are sailing along, things are hunky dory, and BOOM!, something terrible slams into you. Hard. Nothing is okay. And it might never be okay again.

In that moment, you are suspended. You are the

victim, yes, but you are not processing anything. Your body is in survival mode. And you might not fully process the experience for several years. It takes time, precious time. Healing is hard work.

As a mother, the fragility of life is woven into our subconscious understanding. We can't explain it, but we know how fragile our little babies are. We feel them kicking inside of us, and our senses say, "Protect this!" There is not a more protected place than the womb, but even our own womb at times can betray us. Women who suffer miscarriage experience the ultimate form of grief and betrayal. The child hadn't even left the womb yet, and they were still so vulnerable—vulnerable enough to slip past that thin line from here to gone. And nothing could be done about it. All that potential, all those dreams, all that love, snatched away. And no real roadmap for navigating this strange grief.

When I suffered my miscarriage, I knew that it was major. I knew that I would be reeling from it for some time. But I never imagined how it would inform my parenting once my children did come along. And how that trauma, that sudden and serious loss of my child's life and almost my own life, would change how I responded to any future information I would receive about anyone else's trauma.

I can't just read people's status updates and think "that's too bad for them." I feel that tragedy in a deep, deep place. I join them in their grief. I was operating in safety-net mode because I had been sideswiped by trauma and loss. I told myself that if I lived in expectation of it, then I wouldn't be surprised the next time it (inevitably) happened. But this, my friends, is no way to live.

That is the crazy thing about anxiety. When you are deep in it, you are truly convinced that it is the most sensible way to live. The rest of those calm, collected people are actually the crazy ones, because they aren't going to be prepared when their trauma, whatever it is, steamrolls them. But you will. Because you are walking around just waiting for it. And every story of loss or tragedy just confirms what you already knew—that life is just one thin, ultimately permeable line between joy and absolute despair. So you live in that despair, and you resign yourself to staying in that dark place. At least there, you are prepared. Your gloves are on. You won't be caught off guard.

Fear and anxiety are two different things. Fear is an innate, evolutionary response to an *actual* threat. Fight or flight is what kept our ancestors from being eaten by sabertooth tigers. It kept humanity alive. In contrast, anxiety is a constant state of fight or flight without an inherent threat. But, you reason, maybe it could be there. It happened, and it might happen again. So we walk around expecting the worst. Take this, and combine it with postpartum hormones, "mama bear" instincts, a screaming infant, and sleeplessness, and you have yourself a big, fat, simmering pot of misery, my friends.

You believe that going through the worst-case scenarios will somehow prepare you for when they come. But this is counterintuitive. Going over and over them in your mind will do nothing except bring you fear in this moment; it will not protect you from what could happen in the next. That is the greatest lie of anxiety: that if we feel it and heed it, we can prepare for the worst by constantly considering the worst-case scenario.

But it doesn't prepare us. Instead, it cripples us. When bad news comes, we are still as weak and vulnerable as we were before. Instead, we should think on things above, not on earthly things. Whatever is good, pure, righteous, holy, true—this is what prepares us. Thinking about the best and most positive thing actually makes us more resilient. Hedging ourselves against potential disaster, trauma, or crisis only closes us off from God, ourselves, and others. We create a cave of protection that we cannot peer out from.

Here are three things I say out loud to myself, multiple times a day:

You are safe.

You are okay.

You are not alone.

The only way to live fully is to live in trust. And to keep trusting when bad things happen. To carry on, in faith, in hope, in trust, in courage. Because anxiety is a liar and a thief. The enemy embodies fear. He lies, steals, and destroys. But Jesus came that we may have life—and life to the full.

Jesus is as near as your breath. Breathe in love;

breathe out love. Breathe in hope; breathe out hope.
Breathe in healing; breathe out healing. It's all there. Just
reach out your hand and touch it. He is near. You are
not alone.

———

Finally, after struggling through the most difficult
year of my life, I began to be experience glimpses of
wholeness. I didn't really understand suffering until then.
I didn't understand that the suffering I was experiencing
was just an extension of trauma that I had already
experienced. Life is a continuum—isolated events aren't
isolated, and I don't believe in coincidence.

After Evie was born, I decided to build my own fort.
But I didn't realize that after having Tessa, that fort
would be both my undoing and my support, all at the
same time. Being self-employed wasn't the answer to my
work issues. It just magnified all the terrible habits I had
before becoming self-employed.

My people pleasing, my saying yes to everything,
my staying up at all hours of the night to complete client
work, thinking I could do it all—this is what broke me. I
could blame that spider. Trust me, I have. I hate spiders,
even to this day. But that spider was a gift. It was God's
way of inviting me into a deeper story, one that I wanted
so badly to run from.

It forced me to ask the hardest questions about my
life and my choices—to wake up, so to speak. *Awakening.*
That word sounds so romantic doesn't it? But awakenings

are hard. They are messy, even ugly at times. We don't have to choose them; they choose us. But we can allow ourselves to be swept into them.

During my time of being very sick and treating my disease, I was able to have the support of an amazing assistant and operations manager who kept my company running while I worked to simply make it through the day. I would crawl out of bed exhausted, take my treatment, and wait for the herxing (or herxheimer reaction brought on by the treatment) to begin. I would sit on the floor and attempt to play with my girls, falling asleep sitting up. I would try so hard to pretend that I was with them in my mind, body, and spirit, but I wasn't.

I was trying so hard not to break. I was trying so hard to hold it all together, until I couldn't anymore. I remember people using the term "cracked" for someone who had gone mad—someone who had lost it. The last thing you ever wanted to do was crack. That would mean the end of you. What would people say? And worse, what would people think?

Hold it together. Don't crack. Don't spill out. Don't let anything look out of place.

But that is exactly what is needed. We can't let the light in until we crack wide open. And that is what mothering did for me. It cracked me wide open. It led me to absolute mental, physical, and emotional exhaustion. I am not blaming my kids for this—they were just part of the process. But the realities of motherhood pushed me to this place, and I broke.

There is nothing like a major health crisis to

remind anyone that "perfect" can actually kill you. At the time, I thought I would die, and at times I wanted to. But what felt like an end was actually my beginning. All ends are really beginnings, aren't they? I stopped caring about what people would say or think. I turned inward, I tended my own body, I tended my own mind. I said no to everything. I knew that my energy had to be focused on healing. I let the light in, one bit at a time.

I had known the light in the past, in fleeting moments. But now I had to invite it in or I wouldn't survive. That point of desperation is where we are met with abundance, even though we can't see it with our mortal eyes. The darkness felt like it had closed in, but my redemption story was just beginning.

There is blessing in the breaking.

.

CHAPTER 10

THE OXYGEN MASK

———

*Every woman who heals herself,
heals her children's children.*

Liezel Graham

Does anyone listen to pre-flight instructions anymore?

I remember the first time I rode on a plane at age fifteen. I sat, eyes wide, listening intently. I knew the information I was being given could save my life. When you are flying for the first time, you are most certainly convinced that you are risking your life. My eyes must have been the size of saucers as the flight attendant talked about oxygen masks and flotation devices.

I have flown many times since, and for years, I was appalled by the flight instructions for the oxygen masks. I couldn't believe that I had to put my own mask on before putting on my child's mask. Before I save my kid's life, I need to save my own? This goes against every intuition

I've ever had as a parent!

However, the longer I've been a parent, the more this makes sense. And the more it applies to all aspects of motherhood. I have seen it time and again, in my life, and the lives of friends: when you put yourself and your marriage first, your children thrive.

I don't mean this in a "it's all about me, my kids can figure it out" way. We love and cherish our kids with all we have, and we do everything to provide for their physical and emotional needs. But I would argue that as a mother, your primary job is not to raise happy kids. Your job is to show them how to be a whole, healthy, and integrated person in the world.

I'll pause while you reread that last sentence.

More than anything in the world, your children need to see you as someone who is fighting for wholeness.

Put on your oxygen mask first.

It is not selfish. It is not wrong. It is the most loving, most sacrificial, and most important thing you can do for your kids. The oxygen mask isn't employed every single flight, but if you find yourself in a crisis, you have to choose wisely. When you find yourself exhausted, resentful, and bitter, put on the oxygen mask. When you find yourself at the end of your ability to express care or concern, put on the oxygen mask.

Making our children the top priority every second of every day, at the expense of our health and sanity, is doing them a disservice. It is laying a burden on them that they are not strong enough to carry. They will disappoint you, eventually. They will be unhappy, rebellious, or disinterested. They will not live up to the standard of happiness that we so unwittingly place upon them. But if you are tending to yourself, your marriage, and your wholeness along the way, you can weather any storm together.

So often we are told that we have to choose between tending to ourselves and tending to our children. But this is a false dichotomy. We can do both. We can take care of ourselves, make time for ourselves, and love our children well. We need to ask ourselves: is this something our kids are asking us to do? Or is it something we are demanding of ourselves?

When my daughters were five and two, my husband and I took our first ever "staycation" at home without the kids. And let me be really honest: it was amazing. Yes, I missed my kids. But it was so needed. Rather than going somewhere else, we got to be us, in our home. We inhabited the space differently. We moved about the rooms in a more relaxed, less chaotic way. Our bodies, our space were just ours. We weren't tending, fixing, consoling, diapering, or cleaning. We were just being.

We talked and talked until we finally ran out of words around the afternoon of day two. I stopped and realized that everything inside my heart had finally come out, and it took two days. After a while we talked more, but it wasn't the kind of talking that is frantic, the kind that is just about the kids, or the bills, or the groceries. It started there, sure. But then it went to what we were thinking about lately. Our lives, current events, and, of course, how amazing our kids are. We talked about what our girls had been doing that delighted us or perplexed us. And then it went to what we were feeling. And then to what our souls were experiencing. It took three days. And at the end, we felt whole again as a couple. And we realized that although this wasn't easy to make happen, we really needed it.

You know what? At the end of that staycation, we loved our children better.

So book that massage. Take that run. Linger over that coffee, book, or long-overdue conversation. Schedule that counseling appointment. Do what you need to be the best human you can. We can take care of ourselves. And we can love our children well. Yes, some time away from them is going to have to be part of that scenario. But they will be okay. And heck, they might even like getting a little breathing room from you. And guess what? You will come away remembering who you are and why you decided to become a mother in the first place.

Instead of putting your personal healing and growth on hold to parent, you can do both. Your kids are watching you. They are seeing everything you do, how you interact with the world, how you deal with challenges, what scares you, and what doesn't. Your emotional world creates the landscape for their little lives. When they are adults, they will move out, but we never want to talk about that part. We don't want to admit that we are actually going to spend the majority of our lives without children in our home, or with adult children who no longer need us the same way that they used to. And how are we prepping for that? By constantly bemoaning that they are growing up so fast? Or by taking the long view and realizing that soon and very soon these kids are going to be able to call foul on our personal nonsense? They are going to be able to tell us what they see and where we missed the mark. They are going to have insights into our failings that we never really wanted to know.

So instead of striving for some invisible ideal, let's begin by admitting we are all screwed up. No matter how ideal your family situation was, there is no person immune to dysfunction. It's not a matter of if you screw your children up, ladies. It's a matter of how and to what extent. And you don't need another parenting book to help you mitigate that damage. You need to work on you.

It's not about being perfect. That is a complete myth that has consumed us and distracted us for the real work of being humans in this world who are raising other humans. Our job as parents is to do the hard, messy work—the work of showing up to our own lives and not using our kids as something to hide behind. Children need to see us try, fail, apologize, learn, and grow. They need to see us being vulnerable and open to forgiveness. They need to see us live, not hide, numb, and cope.

Your kids don't just need you around. They don't just need your time. They need you to be the healthiest you there is. So do what makes you the healthiest you. And if that means not being with your kids all the time, that's okay. Because when you are with them, they will cherish the memories and time spent with the best version of their mom that they could get. And that is priceless. Kids don't need all the time in the world. What they need is presence. And if spending all of your time with your kids disables you from being present, then you aren't doing them any favors.

Have you ever noticed that kids are super sensitive to your mood, energetically tied to you by an invisible thread? No matter how you try to gloss things over or pretty them up, they just know. They can sense it, and nothing you say is going to change that. Making sure that the people who matter most to you are happy and cared for is a big job. An important one. But everyone else? They seem to want you to take care of them too. Friends, clients, coworkers, bosses, people you've never met online inviting you to mailing lists and events. Instagram feeds or Facebook friends that subtly suggest you could be doing more. It feels like a heavy weight, doesn't it? That if you don't keep all the plates spinning and everyone around you smiling, the world might just crack wide open and swallow you up.

You look into your kid's eyes and you know that most of all, they need you right here in this moment. But giving them your presence is one of the hardest things to do, because everyone and everything out there is bearing down. Lists, logistics, plans, people. So many people with expectations. And you just don't want to let anyone down. You want to please. But maybe letting all those plates crash to the ground and deciding which ones you want to pick up and put back together, might just be the thing to do right now.

When Tessa was young, I said yes to everything. Constantly overcommitting, imagining that there was an entire world of people out there looking at me, wagging their fingers, waiting for me to prove how hard I was hustling. I was caught in a cycle of saying yes, and not being able to deliver on that yes, because I couldn't imagine saying no. I couldn't imagine who I would be without everyone's approval. Would I even exist if they didn't say "good job"? In reality, I was letting people down. Myself, my clients, my kids. Everything was broken, and I was skittering around from one corner of my life to another, patching up all the gaping holes with Scotch tape.

When all the plates came crashing down, I realized that people pleasing isn't sustainable for our souls. As a woman and a mother, my constant stance was to be sure everyone around me was okay. But that care never extended inward. Saying no, standing up when something was wrong, or daring to piss someone off seemed like an egregious sin that I wanted no part in. Until it almost took away my life.

For the sake of your soul, your sanity, and your family, recognize your intrinsic worth. Accept that not everyone will like you or approve of your choices. Understand that you—beautiful, glorious you—are loved, affirmed, and accepted, simply because you are. No amount of outside approval or disapproval is going to add or detract from that. Let go of people pleasing. Sit still. Listen to what you need, what your soul is screaming for. And start there.

It is not healthy to sacrifice everything for our kids. For our identities to vanish, to become subsumed by our role. It is also not healthy to believe our families shouldn't change our lives in any way. We cannot allow ourselves to be consumed by the roles that we inhabit, whether we work in the home or outside of it. If our identity is consumed by a job, when that job inevitably ends, we'd fall apart. When our identities are subsumed by a relationship with someone else, when that relationship goes through a hard time, we question our value and worth in the world. The same is true for motherhood. We must fight to maintain our identities outside of our role as mothers, and this does not mean neglecting our role. We can honor, value, and cherish our role and our families while simultaneously protecting, nourishing, and feeding our own individual identity. This will only serve to strengthen the bonds we have with our family members, reduce resentment and anger, and ultimately improve our parenting.

I want to share the many ways I put on my oxygen mask. This goes much deeper than just the notion of self-care, as valuable as that is. Self-care looks very different depending on what phase of mothering you find yourself in. For some with newborns and toddlers, a quick shower or hiding in the bathroom with a piece of chocolate is a good start. But it cannot stay there. It must go beyond the shallow gestures and reach the soul level, mamas. We have to work toward wholeness for ourselves, and ultimately for our children.

Here are some of the big, small, and otherwise inconsequential ways I put on my oxygen mask:

Drop the children off with grandparents for the day

to spend time with my husband (usually once or twice per year).

Take regular epsom salt baths.

Move my body as often as possible. Typically this means a kitchen dance party, home weight-lifting routine, or a long walk in my neighborhood.

Go to therapy.

Enlist the help of skilled practitioners: chiropractors, doctors, massage therapists, acupuncturists, herbalists, energy practitioners.

Read books on paper or Kindle, and listen on audio. Keep up my Goodreads account to see what other people are reading and get suggestions.

Write in my journal when I can.

Meditate and pray.

Block out certain times of the day for deep work such as writing and strategic planning for my business.

Practice grounding in my bare feet my backyard.

Plant and tend a garden.

Watch a series I love on Netflix.

Cook something elaborate that challenges me.

Put plants around the house.

Drink water.

Here's the thing. This list may seem long, but I am no superwoman by any stretch. I am fairly organized by nature, but I am also very easily distracted. I am always ready for the next thing. We all have different strengths and weaknesses, and mine is focus. But to do the type of work I am called to, ironically, this is the one area that I must continue to develop. As I grow and continue to learn more about myself, work through past trauma, surround myself with positive people who are a healing force in my life, and work toward my goals, I find that my momentum builds and I move into greater spheres of wholeness. Then, this, in turn, helps me focus more deeply on the things that really matter to me.

As I continue to find integration, I also move into greater and deeper spheres of challenge. We never stop learning; we never stop growing; we never arrive. Nothing ever stays the same for long, whether good or bad, and the sooner we can latch onto that reality the better off we will be. So this list doesn't happen every day, of course. This list isn't exhaustive either. Everyone's list will be different. My list isn't a prescription, and no one should ever tell you yours should be either. My list is my list.

You have to ask yourself, What do I need? What does my soul need? What environment do I need to be in to grow? Who do I need around me?

These questions are so, so important.

So, what does the oxygen mask mean for you, right now?

What do you need to survive? Once you've given yourself permission to survive, then you can being to ask yourself what you need to thrive. Again, let me encourage you to not jump on the shame and guilt bandwagon. This is not a selfish act. This is the most selfless thing you can do.

This may mean having a realistic conversation about your desire to earn more money, work outside the home, or utilize more childcare. This may be about you scaling back and spending more time with your children and earning less. This may be about a big decision to change your home, your job, your schooling or childcare choices, and more.

Let me warn you, when you begin down this path of healing, there will be so many obstacles—obstacles in the form of old messages playing in your mind or people springing up, whether in real life or just imagined, telling you that you can't, that it's not worth it, that this is silly. But you must ignore them. You must press forward, press inward, and refuse to hide. Come out from behind the role you are playing and stare yourself straight in the mirror as you are now. Offer that woman unconditional love and compassion. Because that's what God is doing. Offer her that and promise her that you won't stop fighting until she is put back together.

Let's start telling the truth to ourselves. Recognize if

you are angry or resentful. Ask yourself why. Allow your emotions—the ones you have been burying, stuffing, and holding back for years—to arise within you. Allow them to get out. Cry them out, scream them out, sweat them out, plead them out, just get them out. Stop being ashamed of them. Recognize them. Honor them. They are trying to tell you something. They are not here to torture you but to teach you. Listen to them. Ask them what they are saying. Give them space and room to breathe. Give your body room to expand and take up space in this world. Allow yourself to recognize the ways that you have been hurt and don't make excuses for the person who hurt you. You aren't responsible for bandaging all the wounds. Not right now. You are responsible for letting the wounds speak.

This isn't to say that you play the victim forever. This is another topic for another book, but we so often stigmatize victimhood that we lose sight of what a victim really is. We are so often told to avoid a "victim mentality," but to quote the inimitable James Baldwin, "Not everything that is faced can be changed, but nothing can be changed until it is faced."

You cannot move forward from hurt or pain until you have owned it as such. This is not becoming a victim and staying there. This is a starting point, not a destination. But if you never start somewhere, you are already stuck. You are already being repeatedly victimized and you don't even realize it. Owning what happened to you, whether it was a big T trauma, a small T trauma, or simply something that challenged you and hurt you, is not laying down and accepting that you are a victim. It is a brave and courageous first step on a journey to becoming the most powerful version of yourself. Naming what has happened and bringing it into the light must happen before healing can take place. This takes plain language, not coded words or things that don't make actual sense. Use your words and say what you know to be true.

Start there, then move into power and agency.

When you are victimized, your agency is taken away. When you recognize that, you regain agency. Then you build on it, identify it, and begin to heal. And once you do, you will move forward with more agency. But you can always and forever name what hurt you. Naming it doesn't mean you are still a victim to it. The exact opposite is true.

Women who are fighting their own inner demons and powers in the world are not playing the victim card. They are playing the prophetess card. They are speaking truth to principalities that would seek to dehumanize them and steal their dignity. And this, my friends, is courageous. Living into this on a personal level is the most important. Until you do this, you cannot do it on a collective level with any success.

God is with you. He is fighting for you. He sees you. He knows you intimately and loves you deeply, beyond measure. He is cheering for you, and even at this moment is weaving people and situations into your life that will support your healing. Keep your eyes open and your mind clear. Pay attention to the ways He is whispering to you and to what He is saying. I promise it is for good and not harm. It is for abundance and not lack. It is for agency and not powerlessness. It is for fulfillment of your destiny and the deepest level of joy and satisfaction, no matter the circumstance. Good enough is waiting for you to just lay down your armor and be.

CHAPTER 11

FINDING GOOD ENOUGH

———

The beginning of love is the will to let
those we love be perfectly themselves,
the resolution not to twist them to fit our
own image. If in loving them we do not
love what they are, but only their potential
likeness to ourselves, then we do not
love them: we only love the reflection of
ourselves we find in them.

Thomas Merton

Even when spending time with our kids, we all have our
limits, that moment when we need to just be done. My
limit is about five days. After five days, I start to get
weird. I can't really see my kids for the treasures they are.
I get snappy and ungrateful, and I need a break. I need
to get away and be without my kids for a while so that I
can truly appreciate their existence. In any other human

relationship, we never spend every waking moment with another person. If we did, we would drive each other insane. It is unrealistic to think that as mothers, we should spend every waking moment with our kids. Can you think of anyone on the planet, even your spouse, who you love more than anything in the world, who you would never want to be apart from? No. So why do we act as though mothers who spend any time away from their kids are doing them a disservice?

When I am able to work a few days a week away from my kids, I become a better version of myself. I am energized and rejuvenated. I have gotten to use parts of my brain that have been dormant for a bit. I have gotten to roll the windows down in my car on the way home and sing my favorite music at the top of my lungs. I have indulged in adult conversation and caffeinated beverages and snacks that I don't have to share. I have planned, created, strategized, and thought about things beyond what the next meal will consist of and who needs a bath that evening. And that is good for me. Because when I get home, I am a better mom. I have a fresh perspective on my role in these precious little people's lives. I can see the forest for the trees. I'm not wandering around in the forest, cursing the trees under my breath. I can see the forest, and it is beautiful. It is pristine, and marvelous, and daunting, and breathtaking. And without that time away, I wouldn't see any of those things.

Granted, even inside of that five-day(ish) period, there are many times throughout the day that I have to stop and readjust my thinking. I believe that is what kids are here on this earth to do (besides, as Jerry Seinfeld would say, replacing us). They are here to be the potter's hands to our clay. So throughout the day, when, for example, my second child has thrown herself onto the floor in utter defiance because I want her to take off the dress she has been wearing for three days straight so I can wash it, this is the moment when everything in me wants to completely lose it. We Pentecostals like to call this "the flesh." My flesh takes over and I have to stop. I breathe. I say, audibly, "Jesus help me." I remember she is a child who needs me, her mama, in this moment, not a complete madwoman. She needs me to be gentle. To be calm. To be loving. And I know that I cannot do any of these things on my own. So I pray. Out loud. Jesus help me. And He usually does.

During those moments, I try to stop. I go outside for a minute. I put on a song and breakdance in the kitchen. I start running around the room and let my daughter chase me. Just something to step outside the moment and remember it is all a gift.

Every mom has a threshold. You may not realize it, but you do. Here is how you know you have reached it:

You feel more resentful than grateful.

Every little thing your kid does annoys you—even the cute stuff.

You are finding it harder and harder to be kind to your family.

You are having trouble speaking any kind words to your spouse.

You begin speaking to your kids as if they are older than they actually are.

You forget how tender their spirits are. You begin dreaming up creative punishments for poor behavior.

This is how you know, mamas. Stop, take a deep breath. And call a sitter. You don't just need a moment. You need a few hours at the least. For the sake of you and your kids, take an escape. I promise, they will be happier for it too. Even they get tired of us sometimes.

So how do we overcome this sense of obligation and move into a life that involves, instead, the freedom to choose our own path? To choose the life that we dreamed of, and if things aren't looking like we dreamed, to have the strength to change them. To take risks, to stay vulnerable, to stay connected, and to dream.

We must embrace our full personhood in the eyes of our Creator. And how do we choose to follow that calling and passion in the freedom that is offered us in Christ?

We choose to no longer act out of obligation. Yes, our children need us. But they, too, are a miracle that God has given us to steward and protect. They will show us magic that we've never seen before. They are connected in a special way to the numinous. They can open our eyes to what truly matters. We choose to turn our eyes to them and love them with all of the energy we have. We say yes to them, every morning, every day, every moment. And we say yes to our calling outside of our biological ability to bear and nurture. We say yes to nurturing our friends, our businesses, our creative endeavors, our spouses, ourselves. We say yes. And we recognize that in Christ, there is no debt. The books are even. The scales are weighted in our favor. We don't have a hole to climb out of. We don't owe anyone anything. Even our love of God is a response that is drawn out of us by His goodness alone.

It isn't an obligation; it is a response. A response of gratitude. A debtor cannot be grateful to his lender, only bitter. We have no debtor. Not God, not our spouse, not our children. We stand—beautiful, miraculous, created—for transformation and connection. We stand, eyes to the One who gives life, and say yes, and thank you.

The good enough mother, the concept put forth by psychoanalyst David Winnicott that I introduced in the beginning of the book, argues that there truly is no perfect parent.[15] I believe that so many of us have been hoodwinked into believing that if we fall short of perfect, our children will be developmentally traumatized, but the science simply does not support this. So much of this underlying (and often unspoken) belief is a major contributor to mom guilt. Maybe if we can relearn what separates perfect from good enough, we can free ourselves and our children from this unnecessary burden?

In the book *The Body Keeps the Score: Brain, Mind, and Body in the Healing of Trauma*, Bessel Van Der Kolk discusses the serious effects of developmental trauma on children.[16] The research and data is clear: abuse, neglect, and insecure/anxious attachments have the power to completely alter a child's personality and life trajectory. Most of us understand this on a very personal level, as it has shaped our stories. Trauma is stored not only in the brain, but in the body. It has a negative impact on a child for the remainder of their life. But after presenting the importance of a healthy and secure attachment for infants, he goes on to say this:

> *Conscientious parents often become alarmed when they discover attachment research, worrying that their occasional impatience or their ordinary lapses in attunement may permanently damage their kids. In real life there are bound to be misunderstandings, inept responses, and failures of communication. Because mothers and father miss cues or are simply preoccupied with other matters, infants are frequently left to their own devices to discover how they can calm themselves down. Within limits this is not a problem. Kids need to learn to handle frustrations and disappointments. With "good enough" caregivers, children learn that broken connections can be repaired. The critical issue is whether they can incorporate a feeling of being viscerally safe with their parents or other caregivers.[17]*

I can definitely relate. I learned about attachment theory while seeing my own therapist, and I instantly began questioning every action I had ever taken with my daughter. What about the time I was stuck in traffic and couldn't get home to feed her in time? What about our "sleep training" efforts with nights spent standing at the door with a timer, while we listened to her desperate and excruciating cries, all in an attempt to get her to sleep on her own? The guilt was overwhelming. I couldn't go back and change my choices in those moments. Most of the moments were either situations out of my control or attempts to control outcomes in my very early stages of parenting (boy, have I learned a thing or two about control since then). Was my incompetence or inexperience traumatizing my child?

Every single time I met with another mother, she expressed this same exact fear. She simply wasn't sure if she could trust her own decisions. She read every book, every article, and every parenting forum. She had advice coming from all directions—her pediatrician, her parents, her friends, long-lost aunts and cousins, moms in social media threads. But she still wasn't sure that anything she was doing was right. She worried constantly that she was somehow damaging her child psychologically. Her mistakes haunted her, constantly reminding her that she simply wasn't cut out to be this baby's mother.

Enter the good enough mother theory.

It isn't simply about meeting your child's basic needs but trusting yourself to do so. According to Charles Sharpe in his assessment of Winnicott's research, this mother "learns best how to look after her baby not from health professionals and self-help books but from having been a baby herself."[18] Wow. What a novel idea. Mothering from our own intuition. Trusting ourselves. Listening to our gut.

The good enough mother also knows that to meet

the child's every single need simply is not a healthy way to introduce them to the realities of life. Sharpe goes on to reflect on Winnicott's research, "To achieve this shift from the baby's total dependence to relative dependence the good enough mother has, by a gradual process, to fail to adapt to her baby's needs in order that the baby can begin to learn to tolerate the frustrations of the world outside of himself and his mother."[19]

As I began to research further, I saw my own natural inclinations being spelled out in black and white. I wanted to provide the most secure attachment possible for my children, and I knew that 99 percent of the time I did that. I also felt confident that I was emotionally attuned to my babies and continued to learn their cues and needs as they grew. But so much of mothering felt like a constant push/pull, following my daughter's lead, listening, paying attention to her cues, and at times taking the lead myself to guide her toward the best possible scenario for us both. In the early days, this revolved a great deal around the two basic needs (for both of us)—sleep and food. But now that she is older, I see this ongoing tension and balance continuing to play out on a daily basis.

It has been a long process and involved a great deal of healing on my own part. But now I feel that I can say with confidence that, no, I have never "Big T" traumatized my kids. Yes, I have made mistakes. Big ones. I've lost my temper, my patience, and my sanity at times. But my kids know they are loved and safe. I am not only good enough, but I am the best possible mother my girls could ever need.

Respecting the gravity of childhood trauma means being clear about what it is, and what it is not. Neglect and abuse are never okay, and making light of them does a disservice to anyone who has actually endured them. Sometimes parents find themselves in situations where they simply cannot be the best parent possible. They may be walking through grief or dealing with their own trauma that causes them to be less emotionally available. This is the reality of life. After my second daughter was born, I endured a deep, deep depression. I couldn't have changed this scenario, and although I am sad about what that season stole from my ability to experience joy with my daughter, I know that she always felt loved and protected in the midst of it. Humans are fragile but resilient. We are wired for healing and connection, if we will allow it.

As we mother, as we heal, and as we love our children and ourselves, can we make each other a promise? Can we promise that from now on we will proud of being good enough? That we will ditch the perfectionism, guilt, and fear that is trying so hard to drag us down? That we will quiet the voice inside that tells us we are failing our kids and know that we are doing the very best we can with what we have, right now? That we will trust our instincts? That we will continue to work on our own healing so that we can be the best possible mothers to our precious babies?

Does any of the following sound familiar? Your feet hit the floor reluctantly, but you smile. Even though your eyes are heavy with sleep and your mind is foggy with "what day is it anyway?" you know you have so much to be thankful for. You kiss your babies, smell their sleepy heads. You jostle them out of jammies, carefully handle smelly diapers before your senses have even awakened, and negotiate clothing decisions. You put on the coffee or tea and inhale the aroma with greed, knowing this cup will give you what you need to at least get through the morning.

Then once you are fully awake and your mind begins to churn, you hear:

"You woke up at a deficit. Just go back to bed and start over. Wait, never mind... you can't."

"There is so much to do today. You'll never get it all done."

"Today is going to be like every other day. Nothing ever changes."

"That breakfast isn't nutritious enough. Why don't you care about your kids' health?"

"Why were you so harsh with him just now? He can tell you are angry. You are hurting him. You are a bad mom."

"Why don't you get up earlier so you can have alone time before the kids wake up? Most moms do this. Why can't you?"

"Your house is always a wreck. Why do you even bother? The work never ends anyway."

"You aren't enough for these kids. They deserve better than you."

"You'll never have what she has."

Do any of these sound familiar?

These words are not just half-truths. They are not "helpful reminders" of how you need to improve as a woman and mother.

They are one thing and one thing only: lies.

And the only way I know how to combat lies is with truth. Here are some specific affirmations for you to repeat to yourself throughout the day to help silence the voice that tells you that you aren't enough.

I am exactly who my children need, right now in this moment. I acknowledge my faults and shortcomings and recognize that I am growing as my children grow. I choose to extend grace to myself today.

I am doing the very best that I can with the resources and knowledge that I have, and that is the most loving thing I can do for my children today.

I choose to ignore what other people are doing or buying and focus on the beauty and gifts within my own life. I choose to cultivate gratitude for where I am, right now in this moment.

I choose to connect my head to my heart and pay attention to my emotions and my body. I will listen to myself and heed my body's signals so that I can be healthy, whole, and give the best of myself to my family and my work.

I choose to love and care for my children from a place of abundance, not of lack.

I will do my very best to notice the singular magic that this day can hold, even if it's in the smallest and most unexpected things.

I will strive to act in love, patience, and kindness toward my children, and when I don't, I will ask for forgiveness. But most importantly, I will forgive myself.

I will stay true to my priorities in this season of my life and say yes and no without guilt or regret.

I will say no to perfectionism—in myself and in my children. I will say no to striving. I will say yes to being, listening, learning, and discovering.

CHAPTER 12

BECOMING GOOD ENOUGH

———

God can do anything you know—far more
than you could ever imagine or guess or
request in your wildest dreams! He does it
not by pushing us around but by working
within us, His Spirit deeply and
gently within us.

Ephesians 3:20, MSG

In this final chapter I am going to get super practical
and offer some activities and exercises that can help you
on your journey toward embracing good enough. Aren't
you glad you stuck around? Hear me when I say, this
chapter is not a prescription. It is simply an offering,
another woman saying "I've been there, and this is what
helped." If it resonates with you, run with it. If it doesn't,
that's okay. All you will need is a pen, a journal, and a
little time.

REMEMBERING YOU

Before you embark on this journey of becoming good enough, you have to go backward. Or should I say, *inward*. You have to ask yourself who you are, and who you were before you became a mother. I know that's hard to remember some days. I can barely remember what happened this morning at breakfast. But I promise you, if you sit quietly and pay attention, things will start to appear in your view. It isn't just one thing- it's a culmination of things. Experiences, synchronicities, convergences, people you've encountered, places you've been, moments you've felt most alive, compliments you received. Write them all down. Examine them. Hold them up to the light. Stay curious. Ask yourself who you were then. Look in the mirror and ask the little girl inside you what she thinks of you now. Are you where you thought you would be? Is that a good thing? If it is, why? If it's not, why not? Stay curious; stay in it. This might take a day, this might take months or even years. But you must begin here.

EXAMINING INTERNALIZED MESSAGES

Now you can begin to turn outward. Look around you. Examine the terrain of your life. Not the size of your house, or your car, or your workplace. Examine the environments in which you find yourself operating, and the environments that shaped you. Is it at home? In an office? Where are these places? What do they look like, feel like, smell like? What were the messages that you received in these places? Who delivered those messages? What have you believed about yourself that was told to you by someone else? By family, church, society? Take a sheet of paper and create five columns, representing the different stages of your life: little girl, adolescent, young adult, adult, and mother. Then, in the columns, write down the messages you received at each stage in your life. Who did people tell you you were or what did they tell you you had to be? Write it all down—the good, the bad, and the ugly. And then step back. Take a breath. Heck, take a vacation. But don't look at it for a while. Take some time away. When you are ready to revisit it, I want you to be prepared to mark out in huge red X anything that no longer describes you, or never did. I want you to take out a big obnoxious Sharpie and start marking. When you are done, see what is left.

UNDERSTAND YOUR SEASON

Life is comprised of seasons, rhythms, ebbs and flows, intensity and calm, wave after wave. Right now, it is your responsibility to understand the season in which you find yourself. In college I majored in music, and spent every afternoon rehearsing with the college choir. We were like a family, and when we sang, it was as though we operated as one living organism. When we were singing, we were always aware of the rests. Glorious music cannot exist without those rests in between. The rests, the silence, the white space on the page—those make up the beautiful piece of music just as much as the notes. So, it's important to know where you are on the page of your life. Are you in a season that is requiring much more of you physically, emotionally, mentally than you ever have been, or are you in a season of rest and renewal? Are you in a full-speed-ahead season or a deeply internal one? These ebbs and flows happen on a micro and macro level. As women, we have an internal rhythm that fluctuates with our menstrual cycles. I know that when I am approaching my luteal phase, it's time to crawl into a hole and avoid people as much as possible. When I am in follicular, I am ready to take on the world, with tons of extra energy. These ebbs and flows happen on a larger timescale as well.

Motherhood, especially during the newborn and toddler years, is a highly demanding time of life. It doesn't last forever, but when you are in the midst of it, it feels like it might. Let's say an average season of life lasts about one to two years. If this season of your life were a chapter in a book, what would it be called? It's so important to recognize your season and adjust your expectations of yourself accordingly. If you are a mom to two or three children under five years old, the physical demands on you are high, maybe higher than they will ever be in your entire lifetime, so operating full steam ahead in that season may not be the healthiest approach. Everyone is different and can handle varying levels of stress and pressure, so this exercise is completely contingent upon your circumstances. If you are in one season of life and trying to operate like you are still in another, there will be incongruence and conflict.

So I ask again, what is your season? Feel free to write down what your season was before this and what you expect your next season will be. A few chapters, if you will. This can be with regards to motherhood, creative work, your career, or big life transitions. Once you are comfortable with the season you are in, once you are clear about where you are situated inside your own story, you can gain perspective.

PUT ON YOUR OXYGEN MASK

Next, I want you to write down how you can put on your oxygen mask. What are small, doable ways that you can care for yourself so that you are more available to care for others?

How can you ask for help? Keep in mind, an oxygen mask is for survival. Self-care has become so trendy and commoditized that it can feel like one more thing we have to check off the neverending to-do list. However, taking care of yourself is not cute; it's necessary. When you are in survival mode, the oxygen mask is a lifeline. You have to have it to make it through the next moment, the next day, the next week.

When you make this list, it doesn't have to be things that cost a ton of money. It doesn't have to be fancy girls trips, expensive dinner dates, or exclusive spa experiences. It simply needs to be ways you can make time for yourself. I have found that for me, silence and prayer are two of the most profound things that impact my mental health and well-being, and they are completely free. I spend ten minutes per day. So, remember, don't turn self-care into another hurdle you have to jump over. It has to make sense. It has to fit your life and your budget. And it has to be easy, or you won't set aside time or space for it. You can only create so many new habits, and there is a limited amount of space in your life and energy. Guard that energy with a fierceness. With everything you are responsible for in your life, there will never be a moment when you are not needed. You must create the boundary, set aside the time, make it sacred, and stick to it. No excuses.

Another way we can put on our oxygen mask is to identify who is helping us stay afloat and maybe even thrive. We spend so much time meeting others' needs, but it's important to identify who meets ours. Make a list of what your needs are in this season, then make a list of the people in your life who meet those needs. Who is the person who you know will listen when you've had a rough day and give you a soft place to land? Who gives you honest feedback? Who will step in around the house and help you with practical tasks when you need it? Who are the friends you can count on for a super fun night out with lots of laughs? What groups or communities meet your need for a sense of belonging or involvement? What practitioners help keep you healthy, physically and emotionally? You may discover through this exercise that you are lacking support in one area or another, or you have been completely neglecting an area, or simply white knuckling it. Remember, you have needs too. And those needs are valid. Once you've made this list, write down the areas where you feel you could use more support and ask for God to bring the right people into your life who can support you. Sometimes the hardest thing is to ask for help, but you don't have to keep giving until you've been completely tapped out. Sometimes strength means being willing to ask for help and recognize when you need it.

FRIEND MOUNTAIN

Next, I want you to do a fun exercise I call the Friend Mountain. Today, with social media's prominence in our already busy lives, it's easy to forget that our social circles, despite how many Instagram followers we have, have not shifted that much. In our closest friend circle, we can only maintain around four to five truly close friends at once. Outside of that, we can maintain a healthy relationship with up to twenty people, maximum. This includes friends we may have over for dinner, see occasionally, and interact with in community or social settings. The outermost circle consists of mostly just acquaintances, faces, and names from work, church, past relationships and social media. When we give ourselves permission to stop thinking that every single Facebook friend, Twitter follower, or Instagram DM is an actual friend that we owe something to, we can get clarity on who we should be spending our time with. This is a way of identifying your people, your support system, the people who should be getting your precious energy, in this season. Obviously, this will shift over time, and that is okay.

So, here goes. Draw a mountain. At the top of the mountain is your inner circle. These people are your tribe, your ride or die. These people know all the ugly details of your life and actually stick around. These are the people who have seen you at your absolute worst and been with you through your most glorious mountaintop moments. These may be family members, old friends that you have kept in touch with, or new friends that you have formed a deep connection with over a short period. These are the people you know won't just shoot you a text if something is going wrong. They will show up at your doorstep.

The next circle are friends who are in your larger sphere. You usually don't have more than twenty people in this circle. These people could be good friends, clients, or individuals who you truly enjoy being around but just don't see as often. And last, at the bottom of the mountain are acquaintances, people in your larger circle, friends of friends, work connections, and extended family. Up to one hundred people, maximum.

Now that you have a visual of your Friend Mountain, you should have a better idea where your energy should be going with regards to the relationships that mean the most to you in this season. This isn't to say that you should cut people out of your life if they aren't at the top, (unless they are toxic energy vampires, which in that case go right ahead), but simply that you should allow that to serve as a reminder that you do not owe all of your precious energy to individuals who aren't equally as invested in you. Reciprocity matters. It's not a matter of having hard feelings. It's a matter of identifying who is meeting your investment in the relationship at a level that feels mostly equal to you. People who reciprocate your efforts and loving intentions, who cheer you on, who want to see you win—these are the individuals you need to be focused on.

MUSTS OVER SHOULDS

When was the last time you made a decision? Five minutes ago, right? Maybe you ordered a latte and picked your specific kind of flavor. Maybe your toddler asked for a snack and you gave them a healthier option. Maybe you had a work meeting and picked out your favorite outfit. Either way, we are making decisions constantly. Every single day our minds are bombarded with perceived options. Which brand of toothpaste do I buy? What link do I click on? It never ends. What we need to understand is that our minds can only handle so much. Our decisions are most often made from a much deeper place in our brains—the primal brain. We may think we are making rational, thoughtful decisions. But much of those decisions are actually governed by our pre-rational mind. The emotions that drive that part of our brain are survival emotions. They regulate our hormones, our need for rest and food, and our fight or flight reflexes.

So when we make decisions, how often are we simply reacting? When you are asked to volunteer for something, or take on one more client project, or bake those cookies, what emotion is driving your response? It's so important for us to stop and think before we agree to anything. We must have the awareness to examine our emotional responses and what we are feeling inside our bodies. Often, especially as women and mothers, we may find that many of our decisions and responses are given out of a sense of obligation, duty, or a desire to avoid shame or guilt. Shame is a powerful force, and no one wants to experience a sense of not belonging or being left out. So we say yes to the next thing, and the next thing, and the next thing. And then we look around and wonder why our lives are so overloaded. We're constantly living in the land of should and not in the land of must.

To understand our musts, we must be willing to ask ourselves hard questions. We must be willing to examine our current life landscape, our value systems, and ask ourselves "Who are we in relationship with? Who are we working with? Who are we spending our free time with? Do the activities align with my values? How are we interacting with those people, and why?" Getting to our *must* is a journey, but it's so important. If we don't, we will constantly be reacting—saying yes, yes, and yes out of guilt, obligation, or shame. Obviously, I'm not talking about our parenting here, as that is something we have most likely chosen. Duty isn't a bad thing, and obligations aren't either. It's the way we enter into them that counts. So, how do you enter into the responsibilities that you take on? Do you give knee-jerk agreements so that you can continue to keep everyone happy and placated? Or do you have a strong sense of your musts, and give a polite no thank you when something doesn't align with your values, your purpose, your season, or your margin? We have to get to must over should. We have to be willing to say yes or no and stand firm in those commitments. Ultimately, it is about being true to our word—the word we give ourselves and the word we give otherS.

IDENTIFY YOUR INNER CRITIC

Next up, I want us to visit our inner critic. She's pretty active, isn't she? I want you to identify her. She seems to be constantly with us, replaying messages over and over in our minds, that we often believe that she *is* us. She is a part of us, yes. But this is not a voice that we have to constantly listen to and heed. She is trying to protect us, ultimately, to keep us from taking risks, experiencing any type of rejection, shame, or emotional or physical injury. But she must be asked to take a back seat.

Before we can do that, let's examine her for a bit. If she had a name, what would it be? What does her voice sound like? Someone from your past, maybe? A family member? An old teacher or coach? Or maybe just yourself, a somewhat distorted version of your own voice? When she talks to you, what does she say? What are the primary phrases that she uses? In what situations does she seem to arise the most? Get to know her. Stay curious about her. It may seem that you need to fight against her or shut her down, but you can approach her much more gently. It can simply be a process of listening to her, acknowledging her, and thanking her for protecting you up to this point.

But then we must tell her that her voice will no longer be needed. She can rest now. She doesn't have to work so hard to protect you anymore, because you are safe in the world, safe in your own body, and safe in your creative risks and endeavors. You are safe.

A VISIT TO THE DUMP

It took me a long time to recognize toxicity in my life. I thought it was just something everyone had to deal with, and on some level, it is. We live in a fallen world with other sinful human beings, and things won't be perfect. But when you consistently go back to drink from a dirty well, that's your choice. So we are going to do an exercise I like to call A Visit to the Dump. Take out a piece of paper and find a quiet place, where you won't be disturbed. It's time to offload a few things.

You are going to write down all the toxic situations in your life, whether they involve a person or not. The word "toxic" has become somewhat watered down these days, so let me define it for you first. The term "toxic" has a simple meaning. It means anything that is poisonous. Toxicity is poison. Poison is a substance that usually kills, injures, or impairs an organism. Obviously you aren't ingesting poison, at least to your knowledge. But there are situations where people in your life can represent a threat to your well-being. It may not be your physical well-being, but it might be to your psychological, emotional, or spiritual well-being—which, let's be honest, affects your physical health over time. These people or situations may be ones that you chose or ones that you didn't consciously choose. They may be your own family, close friends, coworkers, or even strangers who you follow on social media. They may be a job you hate, an environment that you are exposed to, or even content that you take in through your phone.

So how do you know if something is toxic to your soul? Start by asking some questions. Does this person/situation invoke fear or shame? Does this make me feel as though I must perform to be loved? Does this make me twist and contort my true self to keep the peace? Does this leave me with a feeling of emptiness, sadness, or simply a feeling of being "off" that takes me time to recover from? If you answered yes to any of these questions, your body and mind may be sending you signals that this is a toxic situation. The poison can be subtle, right? Sometimes we can be swimming in it so deeply that we don't even recognize it as poison. We can be so entangled with the relationship or situation that it is impossible to see clearly. But by simply asking these questions, you will begin to gain clarity.

Write those things down on the piece of paper. And read them. Examine them. Begin to ask yourself how you can extricate yourself. It doesn't have to be dramatic. It doesn't have to be a show of force or even something that you announce. You will simply know that something must change, and you can begin moving in that direction. You can begin to decide what relationships or things in your life need to find a home at the dump. Poison doesn't belong in your life. Get it out so that you can begin to heal and thrive.

IN YOUR FEELINGS

So often we are told not to trust our emotions— that they are shifty, untrustworthy, and that they will betray us. I would argue that this is not the whole story. Our emotions may be variable and circumstantial, but they are not imminently untrustworthy. They are not the ultimate destination, but they are signposts along the way. They are pointing us in the direction of something. They are asking us to pay attention. Emotions do not live in our minds. Emotions live in our physical bodies. And our bodies have a wisdom that we would do well not to ignore. When we are told over and over to ignore and downplay our emotions, we are truncating ourselves. Our minds have so much power, but our emotions are signals, flares that our body is sending up. So I ask you to begin paying attention to your emotions, and allow them to flow.

I tend to suppress my emotions until I am at a breaking point. But now, when they arise, I give them space to process through. I get curious about what they might be trying to point me toward. If it's simply that they needed to rise up and be let out, then that's awesome. But I will no longer block their flow for the sake of seeming more rational, poised, or put together. When you stuff them, they have to go somewhere. And they will, eventually, come out, in other ways, be it chronic pain, fatigue, depression, brain fog, and other physical issues. I purchased an "emotions mat" for my children, and we use it almost every day. Providing yourself language around what you are feeling is very helpful—you don't have to just say "I'm in a bad mood." Ask yourself what is really going on. Are you feeling despair? Abandonment? Disgust? Resentment? Become more clear with your language, and more curious with the exploration of your inner world.

INTERNAL NAVIGATION SYSTEMS

All of us have an internal navigation system. Growing up, I was constantly concerned that I was "doing God's will." This was a huge topic of discussion in my youth group, and it seemed to be something that everyone was worried they weren't doing right. How could we know exactly what God's will was? How could we know if we were in the center of it? This uncertainty constantly plagued me. I wanted so badly to be "doing God's will" and making choices that were honorable to God. Over time, I have come to recognize that God is not up there with a measuring stick, scrutinizing my every move, and chastising me when I fall out of the "center of His will." His will is not a dartboard, and our job is not to hit dead center every time. This would be impossible and, honestly, exhausting. I think the way that we know that we are doing God's will is that we feel at peace with our decisions. That we seek to become righteous, to honor others, to love without condition, and to practice compassion. To shed our selfishness, ego, and arrogance.

To bring forth the gifts that God has given us to serve others, and not hide them under a "bushel" as we used to sing in Sunday school.

Take a few minutes and write down all of your roles. Mother, wife, sister, friend, employee, boss, volunteer, head house manager, chief boo-boo kisser, head diaper changer, chef, maid. Then ask yourself who you would be if you were not fulfilling any of these roles. If something happened to you today and you were no longer able to fulfill those roles, who would you be? What would you be at your core? Where would you situate your identity? Most of us spend our lives identifying ourselves with what we do. And these are important aspects of who we are, but not the essence of who we are. If we are simply "being," what value do we bring? You might say none, but I would argue otherwise. You are valuable simply because you are. You were designed, fashioned, formed, and purposed. You were cared for, fed, changed, kept warm and dry, and grew into the woman you are now. And you, simply sitting, and breathing, and being, and noticing, holds a universe of worth and value. Your value is intrinsic. Stop fighting so hard for it, and simply acknowledge it. Work from that place. Mother from that place. Understand that the people who raised you were doing the best they could, and choose to forgive who you must forgive—for your sake, not theirs. Love them from afar if you must. But know deep down in your bones that nothing you achieve or accomplish will change your inner worthiness. Nothing.

DIFFERENTIATING BETWEEN A JOB, CAREER, HOBBY, AND VOCATION

Eat, Pray, Love author Elizabeth Gilbert has an awesome video on the topic of knowing the difference between the terms *job, hobby, career, and vocation.* [21] When I first heard it, it changed everything for me. I recommend watching the entire video (you can find the link in the endnotes), but I will summarize it below:

A *job* is something you have to have to make money. We live in a material world, and you must take care of your physical and material needs. You must earn money. Most artists have jobs that are separate from their craft or art. Very few people get to do exactly what they want, especially if it's creative. A job doesn't have to be awesome, and it doesn't have to fulfill you- it just has to pay. Give time and the energy, get money. If it's toxic, then leave. If it's killing you, then leave. And recognize your job doesn't have to be your whole life.

A *career* is a job that you are passionate about, and willing to devote many years of your life to. If you have a job that you hate, that's not fun. But if you're in a career that you hate, it can be terribly soul-sucking. You should love your career or you should change it.

A *hobby* is something that you do purely for pleasure— to experience life not just as a producer or consumer. It is something that brings you life, and the stakes are zero. You can try absolutely anything, or you can try nothing at all! You don't have to make money doing it, and, best of all, you don't have to be good at it!

A *vocation* is a calling- a divine invitation to participate in the story of creation in this world. It's the highest possible thing you can do. No human can give it to you, and no one can take it away. God is the only one handing out vocations. People can take jobs and careers, but they can't take a vocation or a calling. Do you have a sacred vocation? What is it? And what is your commitment to it? You can have many jobs throughout your life, but your vocation stays constant. And you can have jobs while pursuing your vocation. It is your ultimate calling and your purpose, and it doesn't go away.

Have you taken the time to identify your job, career, hobby, and vocation? Take out a pen and paper and write down these four categories and what they are to the best of your ability. Which ones have you fulfilled in your life?

As a mother, it can be difficult to know where our mothering fits into these. We are told by some that our motherhood is a divine calling, that it's the only thing we should focus on, the most holy and spiritual. By others we are told that motherhood is a job that can and should be monetized and economically measured out. Maybe motherhood is all of the above. It obviously holds great economic value, despite the fact that we are not being directly compensated for it. Either way, motherhood transcends these categories. It is a powerful shift, the making of a new person. It is not simply a change in role or status. It is the birth of a child, and a brand-new woman into a mother.

As the gig economy continues to expand and people's

hobbies are often turned into million-dollar businesses, the line between job, career, and hobby can be equally blurred. It's important to know that not every hobby you enjoy must be monetized. If it is, then it is no longer a hobby. For so long I thought all these categories had to be the same thing, and it drove me crazy. Writing was my calling, but I needed to make money, so why couldn't I make money writing? Making money doing it would legitimize it as my calling, right? Wrong. Often placing the expectation of earning an income on the things we enjoy and are called to can instantly snuff out the fun and joy.

On the other hand, sometimes becoming more serious about bringing a calling into the light and potentially introducing it to the marketplace can help us know if this is something we ever really wanted to do in the first place. Recognizing that these categories don't all have to be the same is one of the most freeing things ever, and it's important to take the time to note their differences. What jobs are you pursuing? How are you making money? What is your relationship to that job? What hobbies do you have? What about a career? Have you had the chance to discern your calling or vocation? What does that look like, and where are you on the path to pursuing it?

STOP HOARDING TIME (A.K.A TIME MANAGEMENT IS A LIE)

I see this post often on different social media platforms, and it honestly makes me want to throw up.

"You only have eighteen summers with your children. Make sure you make the most of it." The sentiment that we can somehow hoard time and "make the most of every moment" is absurd. We, as well as our children, are traveling through time in this current dimension and have no control over it, no matter how hard we try to contain it in photos, "memory making," or tiny boxes on the internet. It's fleeting and is simply a matter of perception.

How we relate to time is how we relate to everything. For so long I tried to hoard time. I constantly felt like I was running out of time, chasing the clock. I mean, when you look at it honestly, we are always running out of time, in a physical sense. But when you look at things from an eternal perspective, things begin to slow. You realize that life is not a race to some arbitrary finish line. None of us are running in the same direction anyway. You begin to trust that things happen right on time, and trying to force things into your time frame is one sure way to drive yourself crazy and make yourself sick.

Who has ever felt that awful gut punch when you realize your child is turning one year older? They will never be three, or four, or five again? This yearning, this longing is real. It's not something to scoff at. It's our own sense of sadness that life is fleeting. And if it weren't fleeting, would it be as beautiful? I love the movie Groundhog Day with Bill Murray. He is stuck in a never-ending loop of one day for several months. He grows despondent, and eventually becomes suicidal. Would we want the guarantee of eternity in this life? Or does the passing nature of it make it all the more sweet? There is no one who understands this more than a mother to a newborn baby. Newborns seem to change during the course of one afternoon nap. Babies and children perfectly illustrate that the only constant is change. So instead of hoarding time, why can't we simply practice being present in the flow of it? Being grateful for what is? That is what I have been trying to do for several years now, and I can tell you it has given me more peace than ever. The sand is going through the hourglass whether we try to catch it or not. It's going to slip through our fingers, so we might as well simply enjoy the moment, right now.

A HOLY INVITATION

When you are with your children, you see a perfect demonstration of flow. Children are in the present. They are not thinking about what happened yesterday, or even an hour ago. They are fully in the moment, aware, and existing. They are playing; they are eating; they are interacting. They are begging us to join them as we hurry through our day, ticking things off our to-do lists. The six words I try to never say no to are "Mama, can you play with me?" Of course, I don't always say yes. There are times when I simply can't, and I explain why. Adult life can't always consist of playtime, and it would be unreasonable to think so. But that invitation to me has become a holy one. An invitation into presence, into flow.

This applies to work as well. We have been taught that work must be arduous, trying, and miserable—otherwise, it wouldn't be work. But when we watch our children, we see that their work is play. And when we, as adults, can tap into that playful mindset, that is when our true work can begin. That is when flow can happen. That is when the books get written, the ideas begin to spring up, the business strategies become clearer. Stepping into flow means allowing yourself to create space to lighten up. To breathe. To sit and recognize that you don't have to have it all under control. To play.

CONTROL VS. AGENCY

There is a huge difference between control and agency. For the first half of my life I spent most of my energy trying to exert control, holding everything in a tight grip. I didn't realize that having control is the ultimate illusion, and what I really longed for was agency. Agency is defined as one's "independent capability or ability to act on one's will."

So, agency is acting on one's will. Hmm. Hadn't I always been doing that? Sure, in the most basic sense. But ultimately, our own personal agency is influenced by a number of things—structural systems, genetic determinants, sociological factors. I had to come to an understanding that, yes, although my life had been influenced by various societal, cultural, and familial structures, at some point, my own ability to determine my future was still possible. I understood that "acting on my will" could ultimately change the course of my future.

That if there were things about my life that I didn't like, patterns I did not enjoy repeating, then I had the ultimate agency to change them.

Where does God factor into this you may ask? Well, I believe that God desires my highest good, because He is love. The desires He places inside of me are sacred, and as I seek Him, they become more clear and refined. But I can't simply wait—I must act. Humans must engage in an act of will and holy imagination that invites the Spirit to come and make things new.

MIRRORING AND MODELING

Our children need to be mirrored—to be seen, known, and accepted as who they are. This is the ultimate need. Although we would like to think we are "ready" for children, there is no such thing. As a parent, our ego is tested and found wanting. We may find our true purpose when we meet our children for the first time, but we are just beginning to understand it. If learning who we are at our core is a sort of falling away, then children place us on the fast track of personal growth (if we will allow it).

Until we recognize that we are seen, known, and loved just as we are, we cannot extend this gift to our children. We will parent from ego, from expectation, from lack. The beauty of this process is that we grow along with our children. The behaviors we try to manage, the social stigma that we navigate, and the shame that we run from—all of this reveals our true selves working to break free. Our children are connected to their true selves. They are broken and human, yes. But they are closer to God. More unsullied by life. They are intimately aware of the present, of wonder, of joy. They are full of knowledge and innocence and have so much to teach us. Modeling isn't about passing along moral obligation, social expectations, or rules that dictate shame, status, or stigma. It's not coercion, molding, or working to create mini idols of our own personalities or unmet expectations of life. It is about living out of grace and, ultimately, unearned love.

———

Becoming good enough is a process, and I hope the practical exercises in this chapter will help you to begin the journey if you haven't already, in your own way. This process is one of learning but also, and especially, unlearning. As you begin to peel back the layers and discern what is true, I pray that you will begin to see transformation, healing, and growth. I'm cheering you on as I continue to do this work myself.

FINAL THOUGHTS

Good enough. The first time I heard the term, I bristled a bit. It seemed a bit like a resignation, like I was just throwing up my hands and accepting the mediocrity I had always feared. Over time, I began to see it differently, and I hope as you journeyed through these pages, you did too.

It's a challenging time to be a human, much less a mother. We are all battling our own personal traumas, collective traumas, and navigating what can often seem to be a treacherous world. I hope that in my personal struggles to embrace good enough over perfect, you can see a glimpse of yourself. That we may learn that although the details of our experiences may differ, we are so much more alike than we might have imagined.

I hope that you can see that you are so much stronger than you may believe. That you have done hard things before, and you can do them again. That with God leading you and guiding you, there is no limit to the joy and satisfaction that this life can bring you. That your mothering can be a testament to His goodness, and your wildest dreams and deepest longings will be fulfilled. That you can dance with your children and your family in the light of a beautiful day as you celebrate all that God has done and will do.

That you will know that even your most gut-wrenching struggles and darkest valleys were meant for something, and that your precious children, someday, will rise up and call you blessed.

One of my favorite songs is Bob Marley's "Redemption Song." I probably listen to it at least weekly. When Marley wrote it, he knew he was dying of cancer. In a way, it feels like his most important song, a prophetic parting gift of sorts. A final message that we can be free, no matter what powers, internal or external, try to hold sway over us.

Here are the lyrics:

Old pirates, yes they rob I
Sold I to the merchant ships
Minutes after they took I
From the bottomless pit
But my hand was made strong
By the 'and of the Almighty
We forward in the generation
Triumphantly.
Won't you help to sing
These songs of freedom
'Cause all I ever have
Redemption songs,
Redemption songs.

Sing your redemption song. Sing it over your children, your callings, your laundry, your marriage. Sing it over your home, over your sickness and questions, over your doubts and your certainties. Sing it over your friendships, your church, your morning coffee. Sing it over everything. Whatever the melody, just sing.

ACKNOWLEDGMENTS

To Dad: Thank you for teaching me that creating is as crucial as breathing. Thank you for letting me listen to your records when I should have been in bed. Thank you for rehearsing your lines with me, and talking to me about literature. Thank you for your passion for art and the written word, and for always encouraging me in my writing. I love you.

To Mom: Thank you for always making me feel like I could do anything I wanted to do, and for always listening. You have been my champion, my cheerleader, my confidant and my best friend, and I wouldn't be the woman I am without you. You are a fighter and I love you with all my heart.

To Matt: Thank you for listening, for being my soft place to land when things got crazy (which was most of the time), for being my constant sounding board, and for walking this long and wild road with me. None of this would be possible without your love and support. Thank you for always believing in me and cheering me on, especially when I wanted to quit. Love you beyond.

To Dr. Andrew Wisely: Thank you for teaching me that ideas are the most powerful things in the universe, and to never, ever stop learning.

To Jennifer Gingerich: I always dreamed of having a fruitful partnership with an amazing editor, and you fulfilled that dream. I so appreciate the many hours you dedicated to making this book what it needed to be, in between your own mothering and work. You are a superhero! Thank you from the bottom of my heart.

To Jen Deshler: Thank you for believing in me and this project, and for your guidance and wisdom when this book was blossoming from just an idea into something bigger. So thankful for you.

To Paul and Carolyn: Without "my Mondays" this book would have never happened. Thank you for always being there to support our family in every possible way. The love you pour into us and our children is beyond words, and I will be forever grateful to have married into your family.

To Ashley Schweitzer: My partner in all things design and business—my "secret weapon", you are simply the best. Your eye for beauty, how you just know the way my brain works, your ability to juggle newborn mama life and being a badass entrepreneur. So beyond thankful for our partnership over the years. Thank you for making this book come to life in the most stunning way.

To Kristine Neeley: This book has blossomed inside of the contours of our friendship, and our journey as mothers and writers is woven into the spaces between each line. Our countless chats about writing and life while mothering in the mess together have been fuel for me, inspiring me to never quit.

NOTES

1. "Vocation," Wikipedia, https://en.wikipedia.org/wiki/Vocation.

2. Matthew 20:21

3. Virginia Woolf, *A Room of One's Own* (Harcourt, 1929).

4. Rital Rubin, "U.S. Dead Last Among Developed Countries When It Comes to Paid Maternity Leave," Forbes, April 6, 2016, http://www.forbes.com/sites/ritarubin/2016/04/06/united-states-lags-behind-all-other-developed-countries-when-it-comes-to-paid-maternity-leave/.

5. Sheryl Sandberg, *Lean In: Women, Work and the Will to Lead* (Knopf, 2013).

6. Anne-Marie Slaughter, "Why Women Still Can't Have It All," The Atlantic, July/August

2012, https://www.theatlantic.com/magazine/archive/2012/07/why-women-still-cant-have-it-all/309020/.

7.   Ibid.

8.   Drake Baer, "What Multitasking Does to Your Brain," Fast Company, October 9, 2013, https://www.fastcompany.com/3019659/what-multitasking-does-to-your-brain.

9.   Julia Greenberg, "This Year May Be a Tipping Point for Paid Parental Leave," Wired, February 5, 2016, https://www.wired.com/2016/02/this-year-may-be-a-tipping-point-for-paid-parental-leave/.

10. John Kabat-Zinn, Ph.D., Full Catastrophe Living, Revised Edition (Bantam, 2013).

11. https://en.wikipedia.org/wiki/Ritual_washing_in_Judaism

12. Dorothy Fields and Jerome Kern, "Pick Yourself Up," Universal Music Publishing Group, Shapiro Bernstein & Co. Inc.

13. Michael E. Gerber, *The E-Myth Revisited: Why Most Small Businesses Don't Work and What to Do About It* (New York: Harper Business, 2004).

14. "Pareto Principle," Wikipedia, https://en.wikipedia.org/wiki/Pareto_principle.

15. D.W. Winnicott, "Transitional Objects and Transitional Phenomena: A Study of the First Not-Me Possession," Int J Psycho-Anal, 1953;34(2):89–97, https://www.pep-web.org/document.php?id=IJP.034.0089A.

16. Bessel Van Der Kolk, M.D. *The Body Keeps the Score: Brain, Mind, and Body in the Healing of Trauma* (Penguin, 2015).

17. Ibid, 119.

18. Charles Sharpe, "Attachment Theory, the Good-Enough Mother, Womanhood and the Social Care of Children and Young People: Brief, Disparate, and Critical Reflections," Goodenoughcaring.com, January 2012, https://goodenoughcaring.com/writings/attachment-theory-the-good-enough-mother-womanhood-and-the-social-care-of-children-and-young-people-brief-disparate-and-critical-reflections/.

19. Ibid.

20. Shafali Tsabary, PhD, Out of Control: *Why Disciplining Your Child Doesn't Work... and What Will* (Namaste Publishing, 2013)

21. "Elizabeth Gilbert on Distinguishing Between Hobbies, Jobs, Careers, and Vocation," Acumen Academy, June 19, 2017, https://www.youtube.com/watch?v=0g7ARarFNnw&t=161s.

ABOUT THE AUTHOR

Hilary Barnett is a writer, entrepreneur, and theologian. She began her professional writing career in 2008 as a freelancer. In 2011 she founded her content marketing firm, Savvee, which has provided online and print content for organizations in over 40 industries. She completed a B.A. in Music Business from Anderson University in 2003, and an M.A. in Practical Theology from Regent University in 2011. She is a loving wife of 19 years to her husband Matt, mother to two daughters, Evangeline and Tessa, and the owner of a feisty Boston Terrier.

She lives in Nashville, Tennessee.

———

You can learn more at HILARYBARNETT.CO
or on Instagram @HILARYBARNETT.CO

.

Made in the USA
Coppell, TX
23 October 2021